Living In Fear Of

Enemies

**Trenwick House
Publishing**
www.trenwickhouse.com.au

Living In Fear Of Enemies

By

Kathy Howie

© 2020

Published in Australia in 2021 by;
Trenwick House Publishing.
www.trenwickhouse.com.au

© 2020, Kathy Howie

ISBN 978-0-9923514-9-6 (paperback)

Cover image © 2020, João Cabral, Pexels
Cover Design © 2020, Trenwick House

Editor; Rohan Howie

Produced by;
Lightning Source

This book is sold subject to the condition that it shall not, by way of trade or otherwise, be lent, re-sold, hired out or otherwise circulated without the publisher's prior consent in any form or binding or cover other than that in which it is published and without similar condition including this condition being imposed on the subsequent purchaser.

 A catalogue record for this work is available from the National Library of Australia

Acknowledgements;

I would like to thank all the wonderful friends and family that have assisted me along the way to make this book a reality. These are the same people that have given me an enjoyable and somewhat normal life.

To my life-long friend, Kerry Gallard, who helped put my story on paper.

My loving husband, Rohan Howie, who helped bring my book to life.

My beautiful daughter, Maddison, who assisted with the design of my cover.

Kerry Payne, with all the well needed help and advice he gave me to get started.

My publisher, Grant Howie, who put all the finishing touches to my story.

Contents

Prologue IX
1. Early Years 1
2. Abandoned and Abused 7
3. Unwanted 21
4. Mackay 25
5. Jonesy's 31
6. Friends 39
7. Unforgettable 45
8. School Days 49
9. Good Times 53
10. Freedom 61
11. First Love 65
12. Independence 69
13. The So-Called Mother 77
14. More Abuse 81
15. Victoria 85
16. Drugs and Depression 91
17. Sort Life Out 107
18. New Love 113
19. Sadness 119
20. Heart Broken 123

21. Single Motherhood 129
22. Third Time Lucky in Love 137
23. A Chance Meeting 147
24. Murder Next Door 157
25. The Proposal 161
26. More Grief 165
27. Growing Family 171
28. Another Move 175
29. Bad Luck Returns 183
30. Back to Queensland 189
31. The Stabbing 197
32. The Armed Robbery 205
33. The Fall Out 221
34. Safe Town 227
35. Shock and Awe 233
36. Unlucky Break 239
37. Living Life With a Few Bumps 245
Epilogue 253
ABOUT THE AUTHOR 257

Prologue

Some people live a somewhat charmed, happy, and safe life with a wonderful childhood. They have loving parents and grandparents, brothers and sisters who protect them, and are their best mates. My life has been the polar opposite and I'm sure everyone has at least one person in life that has used and abused them resulting in you living in fear of enemies.

This is my story, and it is one of abuse, violence, and fear, beginning at the early age of two, and has been a consistent theme throughout my whole life.

I began writing my story in 2015, when I was fifty-eight and my second son was twenty. When he was much younger, he once said about me that, "God has put [me] on this earth for his own entertainment", and I feel there may be a fair bit of truth in that.

1. Early Years

I was born on February 14th, 1957, on Valentine's Day at that. How ironic, the day of expressing love for each other. I came into this world in a little sugar farming town called Mackay in North Queensland with a population of around twenty-seven thousand people. I believe I lived in a small 2-bedroom, square, fibro shack with timber floors covered in linoleum. There were two wonky steps leading to the front door, which was barely hanging on by the hinges. My brother John, who was two years old at the time, suffered brain damage due to complications from birth. My older brother Barry, thirteen years old, tall, and skinny with light brown Elvis-like hair. When he was older, he drove a grey Morris Minor with a tiger's tail hanging out the back. I thought he was so cool and a bit of a rebel, as he landed himself in a lot of trouble as a teenager, stealing cars, motorbikes, cigarettes, and items from stores. Then there was my sister Sarah who was fifteen years old. I looked up to her as a mother figure, as my mother was never there for me, however I later found out she was far from a role model.

Kathy Howie

When I was one year old, we all moved to Brisbane. My mother drank every day and smoked heavily and existed in her own selfish world. Sarah had to practically raise me until I was 2 years old. My sister was put through a lot of pain with Mother - which is what I call her after she has proved to me that she does not deserve to be called Mum, that is an expression of endearment. There was no motherly love, nor did she even display motherly traits. If ever Sarah was misbehaving and bothering Mother, she would belt her so hard on the back of her legs using an ironing cord. You may wonder how an ironing cord was used back in those days, as normally they are attached to the iron. You could unplug the cord from the iron in the old days. To make the punishment even worse, my sister often had boils on the back of her legs. Mother would strike her so hard it would bust her boils leaving her bloodied and bruised. She would let out a god-awful scream. So painful were the whippings that it had left scarred holes in the back of her legs.

One day my sister was caught playing "doctors and nurses" with the next-door neighbour's boy, you know the game "you show me yours and I'll show you mine", showing him her private parts, as most kids did at that age, and exploring their sexuality. Mother was having a Tupperware party with cakes, biscuits and hot cups of tea and coffee with plenty of chatter and gossip. When Mother discovered what was going on, she decided to punish my sister by standing her in front of her friends and guests at the party, taking off her pants, and bending her over to show everyone her private parts.

'If you want to show off your privates, then I'll show everyone, you filthy little bitch!' she said, whilst poking my sister's private parts with a stick.

My sister definitely made sure she kept her pants on in future.

Later in life, Sarah used to take her anger and frustration out on me, what Mother did to her, my sister would inflict on me much more harshly and cruelly, as if it was revenge for her punishment. I recall one time when I had chicken pox and didn't want to eat my bread crusts, let's face it what kid did, instead I put them under my bed thinking no-one would find them. Sometimes we think we are clever but do some pretty dumb things as kids. Well, my sister found them didn't she. She came around the corner with a vengeful scowl on her face, blood boiling and a wooden coat hanger in her hand, slowly unscrewing the steel hook and she did to me what the Mother did to her. The look of evil in her eyes, the hateful callous look in her expression and she just kept swinging that coat hanger as if I was just a piece of meat and I didn't think she was ever going to stop. The excruciating pain of the exposed and bleeding chicken pox sores was the most painful feeling, suffering and defeated I just cried for days in silence never letting anyone else see.

Another time Sarah warned, 'Don't you ask your mother to go to the store with her, you can stay home with me'.

Of course, I was so scared to stay with my sister, I begged my mother to go with her. Once Mother was gone and out of sight, I knew what was going to happen. My heart started pounding, so loud it was like a drum in my chest. I attempted to hide but to no avail. Again, my sister was standing in front of me with the wooden coat hanger, so, so... slowly she was unscrewing the hook with a malicious smirk on her face. It started again. Sarah began belting me, she just couldn't seem to stop. Her words haunted me day and night, "If you ever tell mother, I'll kill you!". So, at an early age I learnt to live in fear of enemies.

At a small age you have to take it as it comes - you have no choice. Naturally and out of desperation, I fell into survival mode.

I do remember the times I would straddle my mother and hear her voice through her chest, the scent of Rum and the smell of smoke mixed in her breath all mixed with her 4-7-11 perfume. I also witnessed my mother taking Bex powder using a piece of Bex folded paper. It was, at the time, the most comforting thoughts of her and a fleeting feeling of safety. My sister would glare at me with piercing, devilish eyes. I realise now that if she just got beltings from the mother and I got cuddles she could have been extremely jealous of me with good reason. My brother used to tell me I was mother's favourite, but my sister didn't want to see it that way. I guess that's why she felt the need to push me below her and show me who was boss, trying all the time to be the mother's favourite.

My Dad was six foot one tall, a big strong, strapping man with the rugged good looks of John Wayne and a slight hint of a beer belly. He was a typical Aussie who loved a beer, the horse races every Saturday and of course the ladies. He always presented himself very smartly when he went out, with his dress suit and hat on, slightly tilted to one side, which was the typical dress code for the time. The smell of Old Spice and Brylcreem, and as he waved goodbye and gave me a brief cuddle, the manly sweet smell would waft through the house as he left. My father was different at home and in the comfort of our house. He always wore navy stubby shorts and the old *Jackie Howe* navy singlet. My memories of dad at a young age are however vague, as he wasn't always around, however, I will talk more about my Dad later as he re-entered my life when I was nine.

I do have a couple of early memories, as I recall one day he was watching the races on the TV and I was lying beside him with my feet on his lap, he was tickling them, making me go to sleep. He kept stopping and I would beg him to keep going until he finally said that's enough. I was so upset and so I thought to myself, if the TV is not on, he can't watch it. I went into the kitchen, grabbed the scissors out of the top drawer, took them outside and cut the TV antenna cable, the old black twin cable that commonly run up the wall.

When I went back upstairs, I said innocently, "Now, can you tickle my foot?"

He replied, his head red with blood pressure and anger in his eyes, 'I'm going to tickle your arse,' and he smacked me.

Funny thing is, I don't really remember him, or my mother, ever hitting me at all. Maybe I have buried those memories deep in my mind, as I so desperately wanted to believe I had a loving mother and father. Dad later told me that he went to his room after smacking me and cried. My sister belting me was enough. Another memory is of my dad having a prize rooster and some chickens in the back yard. I remember John, my mentally disabled brother, who was two years older than me, and I were playing in the yard. The rooster had flown on my back and scratched me so John, being the protective brother, decided to protect me in his own way and get back at the poor rooster.

He was calling it, 'Here chook, chook, chook,' pretending he had food in one hand.

In the other hand, he had a piece of four-by-two timber. When the rooster came closer, he slammed that piece of wood on his neck and broke it. The rooster wandered around the yard with his head loosely hanging to one side. Dad always wondered whatever happened to his prize rooster which died three days later. John would also twist the chicken's heads as they poked their heads out of the chicken wire and laugh at how their feet would go around, and around, and around. No doubt I was laughing too, however, with a concerned look on my face, thinking to myself, *should he be doing these cruel acts to these chickens.*

Anyway, that is a small insight into my early years and the real horrors of my life were about to unfold.

2. Abandoned and Abused

My mother ended up abandoning the whole family on one of her drinking splurges and left my sister to take care of us all. I remember those days vividly, she used to belt me nearly every day, partly out of jealousy but more than likely in spite of our mother leaving her to look after us. I remember one day, my oldest brother, said to come to the bedroom, laid me down, took my pants off and put a sheet on me. He was sitting on the side of the bed with a jar of Vaseline in his hand. Not even knowing what he was going to do. At that very moment, my sister put her head in the door. She screamed at him, 'What are you doing? Get out of here right now'. She then proceeded to belt ME for it! She told me never to take my pants off in front of boys again. That's how child abuse was viewed in those days, the men/boys could do no wrong with no disciplinary action taken and you were the disgusting, filthy girl for letting it happen. Very confusing world, I was living in. I was three and my eldest brother was sixteen. You would think in a normal world your older brother would love and protect you, but not in my world.

On another occasion, he put me in this homemade rickety go-kart on top of a steep hill. The seat was made from wooden planks with splinters everywhere. It was planks on 4 lawn mower wheels with rope to steer with. He got me in the middle of the road, pushed me hard straight towards a busy highway. At first it seemed like fun and a good idea, however, fear soon consumed me when I was hurtling down the hill. I managed to wrestle the steering rope and turn it hard left straight into the gutter halfway down the hill bringing me to a rapid jolting stop. I looked down the hill and saw cars whizzing by at the end of the hill along the highway. How in the hell did I survive those years? I never saw my oldest brother much, which was probably a good thing given the things he did. However, I am sure he did some nice things, as around that time, I would still view him as my hero.

In later years, when I was three or four and living in Brisbane, my sister told me she had to work to bring in the money for the house. She would have been eighteen at the time. Funny thing is, she was a Psychiatric nurse, I sometimes wonder if she ever belted any of her patients for misbehaving, and when no-one was looking. Dad had told my sister that there is too much pressure on her, working and looking after Kathy and John, so Dad took Sarah back to Mackay. He was under the belief that I was left living with my Mother. How wrong he was.

My mother, a full-blown alcoholic by then, decides to abandon me to pursue her own selfish partying and drunken needs, I assumed, putting me into foster homes. Over five years I was in two foster homes and I spent one year in Nazareth House, in Wynnum Brisbane, for

UNWANTED children. I asked her for my toys to take with me and she told me my Dad had burnt them and once again I cried for days – what a callous, horrible person she was.

I do remember living at a lovely home with Mr & Mrs Palmer. I remember Mrs Palmer telling me to recite my address in case I got lost. It was 100 Station Road, Darra. It was written on my port when I started grade 1. It was a brown leather square port with latches at the top, and a small handle to carry it, similar to a suitcase. I remember secretly crying myself to sleep every night wanting so desperately to be with my mother – why, I don't know, maybe it is that unconditional love people speak of that I never experienced. I never cried in front of the Palmers, as I didn't want to hurt their feelings and I didn't want them to get upset with me. I was afraid that they would also tell mother, not that she would care. Mrs Palmer was indeed a lovely lady. I would help her wash and wipe up the brekky dishes. One day I wiped down the cupboards in front of the sink. She said what a wonderful job I had done, so rewarded me by taking me to the shop down the road and buying me an Ice cream in a cone. I really thought all my Christmases had come at once. So of course, every day I am wiping down the cupboards. She must have realised she made a big mistake, but she did buy me an ice cream about twice a week. Probably the first time anyone had shown any sort of affection towards me. The only thing I didn't like about that was having to call into my Aunt & Uncles place on the way back from the shop.

My Aunty Phyllis, my mother's sister, and her husband George, lived down the road from the Palmers. I had never met them before. I would stop off at their place and they would always tell me to go in to see Uncle George, who was always lying in bed in a darkened bedroom with curtains drawn, and the door would always be closed after I entered. I don't know whether he was sick or just lazy, and I could never understand why he was always in bed. He would encourage me to lay on the bed next to him. He would then put his hands on my bum, upper leg, and inner thigh all the while pretending to be a loving Uncle – it disgusts me and makes my skin crawl to even think of it. I would sit their quietly not daring to say anything, as his rough hands wandered over my body, only letting out the occasional little sigh or whimper as his fat fingers touched sensitive areas, too scared to move or run away as this would result in punishment. Every single time I went in that bedroom he would touch me in those places. He would tell me to rub his lower tummy, or at least that's what he called it. In the end I didn't want to go into the bedroom again, but in those days, everyone used to make you do things you didn't want to do anyway. The words 'Don't tell, or else' were very prominent in my life as a child. You did what you were told, whether you liked it or not, and then were told to say nothing. Perhaps that's where the phrase 'Children should be seen and not heard' comes from.

Still I had very fond memories of the Palmers until tragedy struck. I recall one night there was a big storm with lightning and thunder and Mrs Palmer lent on a bed with her knees to shut the aluminium louvers and there was the loudest clap of thunder, immediately followed by the biggest flash of lightening. The lightning hit and it lit up the louvers and the room as she was closing them. She suddenly collapsed on the bed in front of me motionless. I ran screaming to her husband for help. That is the last memory I have of living there. I hope she didn't die. I stayed with the Palmers until I was seven and a half and then I was moved again after that tragic incident. Following that, I have a very vague memory of being on a train with John, by ourselves, I would have been seven and he was nine, and some stranger was picking us up at the other end. We both got excited as we thought it might be Mother, or so we thought.

I ended up at Mr & Mrs Gordon's, but unsure how I got there. I think they may have been the ones to pick us up at the train station. I don't recall John staying there. I didn't really know where John went from there. I think this is when he ended up in the Bush Children's Home. Mr & Mrs Gordon ... yeah, well, here I go again. They seemed really nice to start off with and there was nothing to suggest they would cause me any harm. By now I was really good at hiding my emotions. One of those emotions was I was really missing my mother – why, to this day I have no idea, only that a daughter yearns for her mother to hug her, make her feel safe and that everything is OK. I used to cry myself to sleep a lot, but would not let anyone know, or cry in front of anyone. By now I was too scared to even look at people in fear of reprisal. I just used to smile to everyone and pretend everything was OK. I don't know why I did that; I think I thought if I was good my Mother would come and get me. Looking back now, I think, *what a stupid idiot I was for thinking she would save me*; however, I believe that's the only thing that got me through was the hope that maybe one day she would rescue me from my living hell. I feel now I must have been a very brave little girl. Anyway, back to Mr & Mrs Gordon.

Mr Gordon had olive skin and worked night shift, sometimes leaving for work at midnight. He had a big aluminium lunch box. Something tells me he worked for the railways. My experience there was terrible. At the age of seven my birthday was going to be so great. Mrs Gordon said I could have a birthday party on the day of my birthday after school. But she said, do not invite anyone from school, but I was so excited to have my first birthday party that I did what I thought would be wonderful, however, it turned out to be a mischievous thing. Any form of excitement that brightened my once dark and dreary childhood was worth having a go at.

I invited nearly the whole class. Thinking to myself, it is not a party if I don't have my friends there and surely Mrs Gordon wouldn't mind once she saw my expression of joy and happiness and the excitement of my friends. So, on my birthday after school I eagerly sat on the steps out the front wearing my Sunday best, waiting for my friends to turn up. All my friends started turning up one at a time surprisingly with presents I might add, and I was so blissfully happy. I thought Mrs Gordon would understand and allow me to continue with the party however, Mrs Gordon told me to tell everyone to go home because she was not having a party for me anymore and never intended to have one.

I remember feeling so, so, so embarrassed and upset. My first friend turned up, so I was anxiously opening her present. It was a beautiful desk clock, which folds up into a little square. It was green in colour. Mrs Gordon told her to take it back, so I couldn't have that. I cannot, to this day, fathom why she did that. Maybe she just wanted a party with her and her husband and me and I was the entertainment. I didn't want to go to school the next day as I spent the night crying in my bedroom in solitude with no one to console me.

Mr Gordon used to take me downstairs to this huge backyard and in the middle was a massive Mango tree. He would perch me on a branch, which felt like a kitchen scourer or Steelo pad rubbing on my legs. He would take my pants off at the same time dropping his trousers to his ankles. The bastard would then open my legs and play with my private parts and perform oral sex on me. I would look up at the sky or tree-tops, so I didn't have to see the top of his disgusting, sweaty, bald head. He would get so excited he would masturbate at the same time and make moaning and groaning noises. I was trying to hang on to this branch as tight as possible so I wouldn't fall, that would have resulted in a belting for interrupting his pleasure. He was extremely rough and the branch would scratch the back of my legs and he would make me so sore down there. It hurt me so much, but I dare not complain or even cry. He would then pull up his pants, look at me with distain and told me never to tell anyone, EVER, OR I WOULD KNOW IT! It made me feel so desperate for my mother and I would do anything to make that happen. So, I devised a cunning plan or so I thought.

One day I was at Mrs Gordon's place and I was feeling really sad, unloved, and depressed. I went to school and I had a little key to my port, so I pretended to my friends that I had swallowed the key. I put the key to my mouth so they could also see it, placed it in my mouth and expertly pretended that I swallowed the key. The kids were saying, oh no, you swallowed the key. I thought they would feel sorry for me, what a dickhead I was, however I pressed on with my plan.

'I'm telling the teacher on you,' they said.

'No, don't tell the teacher, I will be in trouble,' I said.

The children still ran to the teacher and told the teacher I had swallowed the key. The teacher, in her wisdom, decided to send me home and promptly told Mrs Gordon about the key. Mrs Gordon said I have to take you to the hospital.

She said, 'Why would you do that you stupid little girl?'

In my naïve, hopeful mind I was thinking, if I go to the hospital my Mother's going to have to come, isn't she? At this point I had stashed the key into my pants thinking to myself, *I have to swallow this key now before I get to the hospital or I am in the shit*. I was trying to swallow it but kept gagging at every attempt. Mrs Gordon and I went to the bus stop to get to the hospital, and at this point I still hadn't swallowed the key. I was twirling around and around the electricity pole hanging on by one hand, when I was out of site, I quickly retrieved the key from my pants and tried to swallow it again. Do you think I could swallow it?

It wouldn't go down again, gagging at every feeble attempt and the task becoming increasingly harder with each attempt. I had no choice but to swallow this bloody key, otherwise I would be proven to be a liar and I didn't want that because I know what that means - punishment. When the bus came, I took it back out of my mouth and put it back in my nickers. I nervously boarded the bus not making eye contact with Mrs Gordon in fear of exposing my ruse. We go all the way to the hospital. I am desperate to swallow this goddam key or the Doctor will know I am lying if they X-ray me. I tried again to swallow it as I walked behind Mrs Gordon with the same result. Simple task: swallow a small key, I kept thinking, still I couldn't swallow it so when I got to the front door of the hospital, I tossed it in a drain on the way in thinking if they can't find it then they would have to believe me. Desperate times call for desperate measures. We go in and the Doctor said we need X-rays, *Oh no, I am in trouble now.*

Mrs Gordon looked at me with inquisitive eyes and said, 'Are you sure, are you sure, you swallowed that key?'

'Yep, I swallowed the key,' I said.

What the hell is wrong with me, I am still lying, I can't believe it, oh well I've gone this far may as well go all the way, probably going to get belted either way and remember I am still thinking my mother will come and get me. So, they took the X-rays, and I came out.

The Doctor said, 'You didn't swallow the key, did you?'

The ruse was over but bloody hell, guess what I said foolishly, 'I did, I did swallow the key.'

I am still lying, still believing mother will come storming through the door at any moment. Mrs. Gordon is looking at me with a scornful expression and thinking, *Oh My God, she is trouble.* She took me home on the bus with not a word. I knew I was in real deep trouble now, and hoping the bus would break down. I really thought my Mother was going to come and get me from the hospital, however, true to form, disappointed me again. To this day I never knew whether they had let her know or not. Mrs Gordon wasn't happy with me, and I don't recall what punishment I received. Probably another visit from George and a memory I have blocked.

I distinctly remember one Christmas Eve going to bed excited but not expecting much, I was asleep, and that bastard, Uncle George, entered my room and woke me. He started talking to me about Santa and he told me if I didn't perform certain sexual acts on him, then Santa wouldn't bring me anything. He forced me to grab his penis and made me perform oral sex, which at the time, I knew was wrong and absolutely disgusting but had no choice or control. The next morning Santa did leave me something. He left me one present and it was this beautiful peg doll with a hula skirt. It was so pretty. Come on, a peg doll!

I think back now, and it horrifies and sickens me to think that he thought that would compensate for his disgusting and perverted crime. However, at the time, being a child, I just naturally thought this is what all children had to do. Wasn't it? This was what I had to do to get rewarded and just thought no-one talked about it.

It certainly wasn't something we compared or discussed in the school yard. God forbid anyone found out.

Every night I would lay in bed awake, waiting, scared, *here he comes again*. I could hear the fat bastards' feet attempting to sneak down the hallway to my bedroom. The most awful sound of my childhood because I knew the devil was coming. My heart pounding, body shaking. I was pretending to be asleep, but my chest and body were heaving so hard it caused the covers to move and the more I tried to control my shaking, the worse it got and the closer his feet came I am thinking, *'He must know I am awake, but I hope he doesn't'.*

Then the silence, and I would feel the covers move, I would freeze, and he would touch my legs under the covers. I would shut my eyes, and in my mind, I would pray, *'Oh God, please go away'*. Much like my mother, God wasn't much help either. Anyway, the bastard doesn't go away, and his filthy hands creep up my legs towards my inner thigh and vagina, so I pretend he has woken me up. I tell him I am tired, but he doesn't give a shit about me, as he just wants to satisfy his urges. Oh well, at least I am not up a tree this time, struggling to hang on to a branch and scared to lose my balance. It is 11 o'clock I think. I had been learning to tell the time so I know it wouldn't be long before he has to go to work at midnight. He has a fondle and a play with me down below, with my private parts, then rushed off to the toilet. Thank Christ he was gone, and I would curl up in the foetal position under the covers, sore from his rough touch and cry. I often wondered what he did in the toilet because he used to moan and groan. At one time I thought he was crying – how stupid of me. Of course, I know now what was really happening in there, the filthy pig.

One day, when we were back at school after Christmas, a girl bought in her big bride doll that she had got for Christmas. It was 3 feet high and you walked with it and it had the most beautiful, happy face. I remember to this day, looking at her, and thinking, *I wonder what she had to do to get that*. At times I wished I was that doll with a beautiful happy face, and no feelings, and no one could hurt me.

The very same Christmas I also got a swim tube from Mr & Mrs Gordon. It was beautiful. Blue on the bottom and clear on the top with fish painted on it. I loved it so much. It was very pretty and made me happy. Anyway, that was short lived as I didn't have it for long.

One day Mrs Gordon was out shopping, and Mr Gordon pounced and took his opportunity again. He removed my pants once again and laid me on a bed positioned in a bay window with a sheet over us. He was making me perform certain acts upon him when Mrs Gordon came home and lifted up the sheet and was shocked to see what was going on. I immediately felt overwhelming relief and thought, *Thank you, thank you, thank you I am saved*. How wrong I was. With that same scornful expression, Mrs Gordon screamed at me and called me a dirty little slut and a filthy bitch. I really wanted to tell her everything. That he removed my pants, he forced me to do this, I didn't do it nor ask for this. What was that I said earlier, let me see, "Don't tell, or else". I cannot recall, but I don't think at any stage did she chastise or question her husband so I guess she was either scared of what retribution she might face or didn't want to believe it. As was the philosophy of the time; let's just sweep that under the carpet.

I am sixty-three years old now, as I near the end of

writing this story, and feel quite disgusted in myself for even talking about it. Now I know none of this was my fault, and I need to express my thoughts and emotions about what happened to me. This man, George, I reckon was about sixty years old then. He is probably dead by now and if he isn't, I would love to confront him to see the look on his face. I really hope he has suffered badly throughout the remainder of his life and if he has died, had a long, painful, and miserable death. Not very Christian of me, but I have no sympathy for this man. I often think if he had time to reflect about what he had done to me, and possibly other little girls. I feel though, he wouldn't feel any remorse or have any sympathy for me or anyone else.

Mrs Gordon said, 'I am calling your Mother. You can get out of here I don't want any filthy sluts in my house sullying my home and reputation.'

I was absolutely shocked, however, I actually started to get slightly excited, I am thinking, *What? See my mother again? Finally!*. I was packing faster than ever, stuffing clothes into my port and I had an overwhelming feeling of joy and jubilation as I was finally escaping my hell. I asked her could she please get my swim tube off the big brown wardrobe for me as I couldn't reach it.

She said, 'You are not getting any of your toys, you filthy whore.'

That hurt me so much and instantly wiped away my excitement, as once again my toys, which were my childhood sanctuary, were gone again. But hey my mother is coming. No toys and one pair of shoes to last

Kathy Howie

forever. She let me keep my shoes because I had them when I arrived there. The only pair of shoes I had. I loved my shoes, they were shiny, black pointed, patent leather shoes with a strap and silver buckle. No-one was taking them off me. My mother picked me up that day and I thought we would live together happily ever after. Yeah right!!

From one horror to another.

3. Unwanted

I jumped in the car with Mother, too nervous to say too much, as she was angry with me. I didn't want to make the situation worse in case she would dump me in some hell hole again. Sure enough, I only saw her for about an hour before she did dump me at another place.

We pulled up out the front of this huge building and she dragged me out of the car, walked me up these huge stairs with tiered lawns either side, towards a massive brick building. There were huge stain glass windows, and we went through these ginormous doors at St. Nazareth House, Brisbane. She had the audacity to take me in there, a home for unwanted children. I had to wait out the front of an office while my mother spoke to the Nun. 'UNWANTED' – terrible word, but accurate. At the time I just had to take life as it comes, god forbid I would express my feelings. That usually comes with Punishment. Seen and not heard, remember. Mother then swiftly left, and I didn't see her again for some time, no goodbye.

Kathy Howie

I must admit when mother left me there, I vaguely remember thinking there are no men here, so I should be safe and not get hurt like that anymore, just a heap of Nuns. I didn't realise there were priests there. The nuns were really lovely. I loved the smell of their clean and crisply starched habits.

Our sleeping quarters were long rooms with about forty single beds running the length of the room, twenty on each side, evenly spaced. Neatly made with stiff blankets and starched sheets tightly and neatly tucked in. I thought immediately no privacy to cry to sleep. I remember every Wednesday a Nun would take us to the playground out the back, we would line up, and then we would have to kneel and lean over her. She was sitting on a chair and we would have to kneel on the ground, and she would check us for nits.

Every morning we had to make our own beds then go to the kitchen and make our own breakfast, all before six am. We would go downstairs to the church chapel and pray for half an hour. Didn't do me much good. We had school during the day and there were only about ten kids in my class. There was one day where it was my turn to hand out the boiled lollies to the kids, which was used as a reward if they got their work right. The lollies were in like a petrol tin with a wide screw top. I felt like I was the teacher's pet for some reason, as I was always on my best behaviour. I really felt good and happy. In the hall, there was four big wardrobes full of toys, but I did not play with any of them. I do not know why. All the kids would fight over them, so I was happy enough just sitting back watching them play. I had my special corner. I have just realised now, psychologically wise, I didn't want any toys taken off me anymore. Yeah, I'm a genius?

One day I got mail. It was so exciting, thinking a letter or something or maybe a card. I opened it and it was shiny new $1 coin. The funny thing is, I didn't know who it was from. It was addressed to me, no letter or anything else in it, just the coin. One of the Nuns said it must have been from your Mother. PPPFFF! I was just settling into life and routine at the home. I know I wasn't there long, maybe a year or so, before the Mother came and got me again. I know I was nine years old by then, because at the home we had been taught the song for decimal currency day, which just happens to be my birthday, 14 Feb.

The song is:

Out goes the pounds

Out goes the pence

In comes the dollars

In comes the cents

on the 14th February 1966

One day this Nun came and said, 'Kathleen you are going home.'

I don't recall any sexual or physical abuse at the home, however, maybe more buried memories. I do remember there was a set of large stairs going up to another floor and other children at the home said to me, 'You don't ever want to go up there'. Sometimes children would be gone for two or three days and we always thought they might have gone home, however, they would return with a silent despair, defeated and fear in their eyes.

I have since read many stories of abuse at Nazareth House, Wynnum, Brisbane.

4. Mackay

I was all excited again, thinking now I might live with my Mother. My Mother and 2 brothers were there to pick me up. We all hopped in this white Ute. They had already picked up my disabled brother, John, from the Bush Children's Home. My older brother, Barry, was driving. My Mother was closest to the passenger door. I had not seen my brothers for so long and had almost forgotten that I even had a family. John and I were in the middle. Mother said we were going to Mackay. I got so excited because I thought, *there is snow there,* for some reason. I don't know why I thought that.

When we were about halfway there, I got car sick. My mother had grabbed me quickly and shoved my head out the window of a very fast-moving car mind you. As I attempted to throw up out of the window, I seemed to be slightly late or off target, and I spewed on mother and all the luggage which was in the back of the Ute. She was livid. We pulled up at a service station where I was berated and then crudely cleaned up along with her and the luggage. I remember she wasn't really happy about that and more than likely blamed me. She said she needed a drink now, so Barry had to pull into a bottle shop and get her some OP rum. No coke, she just drank it straight out of the bottle.

She teased my hair, and said, 'You have got to look good for your Father.'

She even put lipstick on me. Lipstick, on a nine-year-old!

We finally arrived, after twelve hours of driving, in Mackay, and I asked her where the snow was. Mother said, there is no snow here you stupid girl. I was so disappointed. It was so hot though. (A quote from Kerry, my transcriber, as laughing her head off, 'The snow has melted, let's go find some air conditioning.')

We went to this, what I felt like, was a men's camp, built using portable Dongers, a long line of blue buildings, which seemed to go forever. We pulled up out the front and I remember all the men were peering out their windows wondering what all the commotion was and I could feel their eyes ogling me and undressing me. I was so scared by now as this is my worst nightmare, a building full of George's. My Mother angrily told John and I to get out of the car, so we did, then she quickly jumped back into the car and told my brother Barry to quickly drive off, NOW!

John was calling them in his own language, 'You buddy bassards.'

I was screaming, and started balling my eyes out, thinking, *Oh My God, look at all those men.*

Barry said to mother, 'We can't just leave them here.'

I can clearly see her face as she started laughing. Sick sense of humour to me, what a heartless bitch. Dad must have heard the commotion and recognised us and came out to the car. With me it was a case of mixed emotions, not knowing what was coming next. As much as I wanted to stay with my Dad, I was so, so scared of all these men, after all the ordeals I had been through already.

My Dad was saying, 'I can't have them here, this is a men's camp with the council.'

At least he realised this was no place for children, especially a nine-year-old girl.

They decided that we would go with Dad in his car to Blacks Beach, where my sister lived in a little square tin shack, with lino on the rough dirt floor. The floor wasn't even flat, rocks were sticking through the lino as the lino had just been placed over the top of the rocks without them being cleared. The windows had no glass, but were corrugated iron doors, and they had to be propped open with a stick. My sister and her husband, Ian, came out. My sister was pregnant with her first child.

Sarah was telling Dad, 'We can't have [them] with a baby on the way.'

Dad said, 'Well I can't have them either,' at his men's camp.

My Mother just said well it's your turn. What a shit show, and that word again. 'unwanted', by my own family. They all talked and argued while John and I were just standing there listening to them all saying why they couldn't have us, never once arguing why they could have us. Like fighting over two pet dogs. Then Mother had had enough and motioned to Barry to get in the car and they just took off. They decided that Sarah and her husband would look after John and me for a week, until Dad found a Foster home for us.

Foster home. I remember my sister taking me down to the beach by herself. I had not seen her for a number of years, however I was so scared of her, because I remembered how she used to hit me when I was little. While we walked, she said she would never ever hit me like the way she did when I was little, and that it was all my Mothers fault because of the way she used to hit her. I was only nine years of age, but I had become very mistrusting and I didn't believe a word she said. In the week I stayed with Sarah, I went to St Joseph's School in North Mackay.

A week later Dad came to pick us up, and he had decided to place us separately at two different homes. John was placed with a single lady, Rita, who I think Dad was pretty keen on. Gave him a reason to visit her, I guess. Dad and I dropped him off there, not easily, believe me. He kicked and punched and swore 'Buddy Bassards'. He didn't take to change very well. Rita said to go, and he will settle after we go, which he did. She was a lovely lady, sweet, kind, and loveable. John needed that I think.

It was time for me to be placed. I was begging him, please Daddy can I live with you? Please, I will be good, I will do all the dishes and floors and I will look after you. To no avail though, as my requests fell on deaf ears. He told me he works for the council and lives in a men's only camp and that is no place for a young girl. I realised then that I wouldn't want that anyway. I said I do not like strange men. I was thinking I hate them in fact, the way they are able to touch my body in the way they wished, and I had no control over what happened to me. Powerless. Too young still to be boisterous and say do not touch my body. I never ever expressed this to Dad.

So now it's my turn to find out where I will live. We drove a couple of minutes. I had trepidation in where I was about to be dumped and we pulled up at this huge very scary dark brown house. It really looked haunted to me. We went up the front stairs with two dogs barking endlessly. One dog was an Alsatian, and the other a sausage dog. Straight up I didn't want to stop there. I was so scared once again, my heart pounding in my neck, but I was powerless, and had no choice about it. Like a bag of potatoes passed over the counter. Dad introduced me to this lady called Jonesy.

Maybe one of Dad's acquaintances I thought. She had such funny curled hair. When she washed her hair, she would put silver butterfly clips in it to make it curl. She seemed pretty scary herself at the time. Then this tall 6ft2 inches, very skinny guy called Benny, came to the door. He smiled at me. He was her son. I thought, *Oh here we go again!* I immediately started to cry. My life stinks. Hope this guy doesn't hurt me, but I thought that would be too good to be true. I thought every man needs to secretly touch innocent young girls on the vagina, like a sick game of lust and pleasure. I just can't wait to grow up so I am in control of my life, my body and who touches me and can say NO, or so I thought. Dad stopped for a while having a cup of tea and chatting with Jonesy. It made me feel a little bit at ease as Dad didn't just dump me there and take off. I grabbed my port unpacked my meagre possessions and my only pair of shoes in this bedroom, which was pretty good, I must say. Dad eventually finished his cup of tea and said his goodbyes and gave me a hug. The dogs actually liked me after a while. There was a Siamese cat also, called Rani. Very pretty. Jonesy also had chooks in the back yard, and I immediately thought of John and what he would do to them. The house was across the road from the main railway line into town. The crossing was two doors down, and across the road. The trains used to blow their horns at one o'clock in the morning, every single bloody morning.

5. Jonesy's

It was very hard to take for the first few weeks. I would often wake up before the train horn went, so accurately on time the train was. After a while you got used to it. Jonesy showed me around the house. She seemed really lovely, with gentle touches, and she spoke in soft tones, which was comforting. Time would tell, however. She had two other boarders, one was a little boy about my age, and a lady called Pat. Pat was a teacher at St Marys Primary School, which was the school I was going to. The reason I changed schools was due to Jonesy's house being on the South side of Mackay, so I had to go to a school close to home. I started in Grade 3, but they found out I couldn't read to the level required, so they decided to keep me back in Grade 3 the following year. I was quite happy knowing that Pat was teaching Grade 4, but when the year started, she came back to teach Grade 3, not happy with that. Getting taught by a person you lived with; so no short cuts on homework. I ended up having Pat for Grade 3 & Grade 4. As for the little boy, Kenny, they had to put him in a different home because those days they couldn't have a male and female boarding together. How ironic, and it reflected the times, as you couldn't have a boy board in the same house, but you can put a little girl in foster homes with depraved, sexually perverted old men.

Every time Jonesy's son, Benny, would say 'Hi', I would say 'Hi' back, very sheepishly and with distance between us, just to be polite and then run to Jonesy for protection out of fear and mistrust. Well, as time went on, Benny didn't touch me or try to abuse me in any way, in fact he was very friendly. In my young and fractured mind, I thought there was something wrong with him or perhaps something wrong with me because he didn't want to touch me. I eventually came to realise Benny was, what appeared to be, a normal man, and maybe in some warped world, not all men are assholes. At the tea table he used to tell funny jokes and he would have me laughing so much I would be choking on my dinner with tears streaming down my face. Tears of joy not of fear; how odd! Jonesy would tell Benny to stop, however, she would be quietly having a little giggle herself behind her napkin. Another peculiar phenomenon for me and new experience, laughter at home. Jonesy was a widow, so no other men to worry about. Finally, a place that felt like a home and where I felt safe, a place of mutual trust and respect, a place filled with love and not fear, however, I was always on guard.

One year later, Jonesy asked Benny to build a cubby house underneath the main house for me. Wow, this cubby had floorboards on the dirt, which was better than my sister's house, and upon that realisation I produced a little smirk thinking my cubby is fancier than her house. Jonesy would go to the op shop to find tables, chairs and even a sink. My cubby house was like having my own unit, albeit under Jonesy's house and came with a small sense of freedom and perhaps what life could be like once I was old enough to leave. It was still very dark down there with spider webs to negotiate, the odd cockroach to shoo out of the way and occasionally a cane toad lurking in the corners waiting to pounce on my foot. As excited as I was about having a cubby house, I didn't play in it very much. Whilst it offered some freedoms the darkness of the cubby and the solitude would elevate a lot of my fears. The walls were constructed of wooden lattice work. Benny even built a kitchen hutch for my cups and plates. They made me feel like a princess and provided me comfort, safety, and a relatively normal childhood.

I just had to get used to not asking to go to the toilet every time, as I still felt it wasn't my home. I would always ask Jonesy, 'May I please go to the toilet?'. Jonesy would say, 'You don't have to ask, just go.'. I think that was the first step to feeling like this was my actual home with the freedom of being able to do something without asking even though it is a simple task, like going to the toilet. If I awoke wanting to go to the toilet, Jonesy would constantly encourage me to go to the toilet on my own. The problem was I was too scared walking through the house, venturing down the passage, that seemed like an endless tunnel with squeaky floorboards and slippery lino, opening the squeaky door and then when I had completed my business, pulling the big long chain, which made the loudest noise with a clang and a flush.

In my bedroom I was always scared at night imagining footsteps moving towards my door and what may enter my room. Nothing ever like that happened at Jonesy's house though. On some occasions, I didn't want to wake anybody up and was far too scared to leave the bedroom. The noise of the chain on the side of the toilet was very noisy and scary and I thought it would wake everyone up including the neighbours. I just didn't want to go there so I used to get into the big brown cupboard in my room and pee on my dirty clothes that were on the bottom of the cupboard. I am not sure if I ever got in trouble for it though. After a considerable amount of time at Jonesy's, I did get a bit too cosy and felt like I was loved, and I asked Jonesy one day if I could call her Mum? She said no, 'You only have one Mum and it's not me.'. I never saw my Mother so I couldn't see her reasoning as she was the only person to show me any sort of adoration and to me was the closet person I had to ever being a Mum. But hey that's life, get over it, move on.

Nearly every Wednesday night Dad would take me to my sister's place and play cards. We would play for hours, Gin Rummy, 500, Euchre etc. At times, dad would not turn up. He would get too drunk and got stuck in the pub, so I believe. Those nights I would wait, kneeling on my bed, peering out of my bedroom window, waiting for his car to come over the railway line and pull up out the front, as I did every Wednesday night. Waiting, Waiting, Waiting.

Jonesy would tell me, 'I don't think he is coming tonight.'

I would say, 'I will wait a little bit longer, he is coming, I know he is coming.'

But he didn't. I would eventually have to go to bed, and I would cry myself to sleep and wet my bed. Jonesy had me to the Doctors about that, and he said it was just nerves. The next time Dad turned up to pick me up after disappointing me on those occasions, Jonesy would summons him inside and discreetly tell Dad, in her stern softly spoken way, that he shouldn't disappoint me like that, and how it was having an adverse effect on me. I loved dad and him picking me up for outings was the highlight of my week, so I would always forgive him and never tell him off, as I thought he would never come back.

On most Saturday nights, Dad would take me to the old-time dances in Glenella, and we would come home about 12 o'clock, however Dad would always have too many beers and would be blind drunk. We had to drive over an old rickety wooden bridge, The Hospital Bridge, with no rails and barely enough room for two cars. One night I clearly remember I had to steer the car as he was veering towards the side of the bridge. I would grab the wheel at the bottom and correct his erratic driving.

He would complain drunkenly, 'There must be something wrong with this bloody car. I can't seem to steer the bloody thing. I will have to put the car in tomorrow to get fixed.' I told him the next day and he was angry with me and said, 'Don't you ever do that again.'

I used to be so terrified driving over that old rickety bridge, and I thought if it happens again, I will grab the steering wheel. Just don't tell Dad. You know when I was scared, I would often think of tomorrow. Tomorrow will be a better day. I always thought of the future. *It has to get better doesn't it?* Dad would give me $10 a week, $9 for my board at Jonesy's, 50c for school fees and 50c for me. Yay! I always bought a bottle of milk with the cream on top and the silver foil cap and a packet of BBQ chips. I loved it. Having my own money and some feeble attempt at some control of my life.

One day I was playing next door with the neighbour's kids. We were playing house and having pretend cups of tea. I said I was really thirsty, so this little girl went under her house and got me a drink, which I thought was water. I gulped it down really fast. I soon realised it was burning my throat and I started gagging and screaming. I ran home to Jonesy's and she rushed next door, and the girls Dad begged the other kids to tell her what they gave me. The neighbour's daughter begrudgingly pointed to the bottle White King bleach. In a panic Jonesy hurriedly whisked me off to the Doctors. The Doctor told her to pump as much milk into me as she could. It will line the stomach and counteract the bleach.

Of course, I sat at the kitchen table with about 5 bottles of milk in front of me. I am thinking, *Fantastic! All I need now is BBQ chips.* Jonesy had a concerned look on her face and seemed really worried about me. Again, that strange feeling came over me of love, trust and warmth and it made me feel safe and that I finally belonged to a family who would protect me. I lived with Jonesy for 6 wonderful and loving years. I am sure there were bad days, sad days, as all kids experience. It was the best home I ever had in my young life. Finally, life appeared normal and I could live without fear of enemies.

Jonesy never had a car, so we rode pushbikes everywhere. Our pushbikes were girls' bikes with a basket on the front and a paper carrier on the back that was like a huge mouse trap. Jonesy would sometimes clean offices at businesses and on Saturdays we would head into town to clean Doctors and Dentists surgeries until about 12 o'clock. Sometimes we would then ride 15kms to and from a Zoo, that was on Harbour Road.

One day she gave me some mercury to play with, which is a bit weird why would you give a kid mercury. Any way I had a signet ring Jonesy had bought me for my Birthday, don't know which Birthday it was though. As I played with the mercury, the ring begun disintegrating to powder. All that was left was the little red gem. So, we both learnt, do not play with mercury. At twelve o'clock she would shout me a pie from Byrnes' pie cart and a bottle of Passiona. We would sit in the park on the grass under a tree together to open our bottle of Passiona with a fizz, and eat our plain pies with mashed peas under the top, and Worcestershire Sauce and enjoy the beautiful sunny day. I would hurriedly eat my lunch because what was next was the most exciting part of the day and week, and I couldn't wait. Excitement how about that!

We would ride our pushbikes out to the Harbour Road Zoo, called Bayersville Zoo. Jonesy's best friend owned the Zoo and allowed me to get close to the animals. There was one cheeky little monkey, and we both took a liking to each other. Gorgeous little fellow. I was allowed to hold him and pet him. He used to de-flea me and try and pick the freckles off my face. I would pretend to de-flea him back. He used to go to sleep on my lap. These were just the most joyful and memorable days of my childhood. I thought how lucky I am, how many kids would get to hang out with a monkey. One of my other enjoyable chores was to advertise the toffee apples. Mrs Ayres would give me a fresh toffee apple and I would walk around and eat it in front of all the other kids so they would nag their parents to buy them one. We would then ride our bikes home in the late afternoon enjoying the cooler breezes and I would reflect on my day.

On another occasion, excitement entered my life. Too my amazement, and with an explosion of feelings like, joy, excitement, and happiness, one particular Christmas I got this two-foot high walking doll from Jonesy. I cherished that doll for many years. It brought back memories of years ago when that girl turned up at school with one and I desperately wanted one. Surprisingly, I didn't have to do anything to a bald old man to get it. Just another moment that made me finally feel loved and WANTED and that maybe dreams can come true.

6. Friends

I met my two, good life-long friends, Crystal and Dana, at St Mary's primary school. I used to ride my bike over to their places of an afternoon after school. Crystal and I used to get into all kinds of mischief. Crystal lived in a low block house with a giant Tamarind tree in the front yard. We would go up and sit in that tree for ages just talking and eating Tamarinds. Sour bitter bloody things they were. She had a four foot deep drain running along the back of her place, which, when it was raining the drain would fill with water.

We would get these big tyre tubes and float down along the back of all the houses in her street. Sometimes we were a bit naughty and pinched some strawberries from the back of a neighbour's yard. Some afternoons Crystal would make me some afternoon tea which consisted of toast, butter, Worcestershire sauce, tomato sauce, pickles, salt, and pepper. Sounds disgusting however surprisingly it was so yummy. Dana, Crystal, and I would also climb mango trees and sit up there, devouring mangoes and talking.

Kathy Howie

Later, I went to Our Lady of Mercy College, where all the girls had come from different primary schools around Mackay. Gorgeous girls, I must say.

Whilst still living at Jonesy's, I decided that I wanted to make my Confirmation, as I was attending a Catholic School and felt it was the right thing to do. I was 10 years old at the time and I advised the Nuns that I would like to be Confirmed and they asked if I had been baptised. I had to go to get baptised before I could make my Confirmation. According to the Nuns, you can't make your Confirmation without being Baptised, apparently. I had to ask my Dad or my Sister whether I was. Well No-one knew whether I was Baptised. I went to the Nuns at St Marys and said I don't know if I have been Baptised and no-one can confirm it. They looked at me bewildered and decided to Baptise me, with the permission of my Dad. It is called Conditionally Baptised.

My life was seemingly everything I had wanted, however, there was always that notion of whether my mother would come and collect me from my utopia and whisk me off somewhere else. I decided, though, I was going to have fun while it lasted. Dana and Crystal would always come and pick me up for church every Sunday morning. We lived just around the corner from each other. I was so deliriously happy, and finally, I had two beautiful friends in my life. We did everything together and talked our adventures and what our life held for us next. Crystal and Dana would go to the old-time dances in Glenella with Dana's parents. I would always meet them there. There was always a very pretty and shy girl down the end of the hall, and her name was Marilyn Wallman. She used to sit with her brother and parents. One night we decided to ask her to sit with us because she seemed to be our age and looked lonely. We had some wonderful nights and memories with her until suddenly one day on the news it was reported that she was missing.

We were all in absolute shock and disbelief. She was missing. How? No one knew what had happened to her and where she was, just vanished. Marilyn had left the house on her bicycle to head down the long dirt drive on the cane farm to the bus stop with her brother not far behind. When the brother arrived, all he found was her bike and school port laying on the ground. Her parents got their whole cane farm searched and ripped up to try and find her, however to no avail. My god this is Mackay, and this was not the type of town where this had ever happened before. I remember it being a very sad town for a long while and parents and children were living in fear. Here we go, living in fear of enemies. Her parents must have been devastated. I did recently hear that they found some skull remains about 30 kms away. It is believed to be those of Marylin. I often think what had happened to her and what she went through, and the thought crossed my mind that that could have been me in my younger days.

When I was about eleven years old, Dad and Jonesy decided to put me into the local marching girls club. There was always forms to fill out for excursions and performances which had to be signed by a parent or guardian. Jonesy would always cross out the parent and signed under guardian, which I hated and was embarrassed about as all the other kids had parents. I would hide the forms from the other children, so they were unable to see them. This was the same for all forms required for the school. I was extremely excited and always had lots of fun with my marching girls and made lots of friends, some of which I often run into today. We went away to different towns up and down the Queensland coast to compete at various Marching competitions.

We competed hard and we won up to seventy medals and I was immensely proud of these achievements. We would experience joyful and excited bus and train trips. We would all get billeted, in pairs, to local families and this would always make me feel uneasy as it reminded me of my younger days. One family where we were billeted, took us to the beach one day. The husband, who appeared to be an older gentleman, was throwing us off his leg into the water and was clearly grabbing between the legs on my vagina. My fears immediately returned, and I thought, *Oh my God! Really! Again! Can't people leave my private areas alone!* I just wanted to have fun. Just when I thought it wouldn't happen again, some dickhead older man has to have a feel. Perhaps it was an innocent mistake, and he didn't mean it or perhaps he did it on purpose I will never know. I had been conditioned to shut up and the words *"Don't you tell anyone"* were screaming in my head, so I still didn't tell anyone. Didn't want to stir up trouble, as marching girls meant so much to me.

One other trip with the marching girls, we travelled on a rail motor up to Townsville, the Captain of the marching girls brought her brother along. Another girl and I slept on the floor and the brother was on the seat. He was putting his hand through the gap in the seat to try to touch our private areas unnoticed. We slapped his hand away and we had to move elsewhere to sleep still scared stiff as I thought there might be retribution. I still loved Marching Girls and there were many more highs than lows and I still have all my medals that I was so proud of.

Occasionally on Sundays, Dad would pick me up and take me mud crabbing or fishing or just to the beach. I did have five fantastic years with Dad, however, I never mentioned the sexual abuse, and the horrors of my childhood to him. I just wanted my times with dad to be safe, joyful, and memorable, as Father and Daughter time. And they were, and sometimes it brings a tear to my eye. Dad would always take a few bottles (long necks) of beer with him. The drives home from some places could become quite scary in the car. *Hang on to that steering wheel Kathy!* I enjoyed the fishing and crabbing, but you always had to be quiet and not venture to far away, which often got boring, but I would never complain. Sometimes Dad would pick up my brother John from Rita's place, where he lived, and take us both out. I love my brother and hugely enjoyed those days he came with us, as I had some company and someone to explore with, but he was always doing what seemed like silly or fun things. On reflection, they were extremely dangerous, and my excitement and joy would turn to fear.

At the beach one day John convinced me that it would be a great idea to bury me in the sand up to my neck. Naively I agreed. Once John had me buried, he would then run away laughing and leave me there. It was long enough for me to think I was going to drown when the tide comes in. I am now getting very scared and screaming out to him and he just kept laughing. John would eventually dig me out once his amusement had subsided.

By the time John was fourteen and I was twelve, he became difficult to handle for Aunty Rita, due to his mental illness. The Doctor did advise Dad that children with his mental condition can change their personality and nature every seven years, either for the better or worse. He had definitely changed although I am unsure if for better or worse. For the first seven years he tried to kill animals, which sounds terrible. The next seven years he loved animals, and wanted to bring all stray animals home to Rita's place. The problem was he was taking other people's animals as well. He even stole the dog from down the road and asked Rita if he could keep it, telling her he found it roaming the streets.

7. Unforgettable

Poor John, I thought I was unwanted. Dad had this great idea of telling John we were going on a weekend fishing trip. John loved fishing and always got very enthusiastic about his fishing trips. Dad came around to Jonesy's place and picked me up telling me we were going away for the weekend.

I will never forget this. Dad told me we were picking up John from Rita's place, and he then laid out his cunning plan.

Dad said, 'We are telling your brother we are going on a fishing trip, but really we are going to drop him off at the Bush Children's home in Townsville.'

That was four hours away from Mackay. I was so upset and terrified for him, as I know what it feels like to be dumped, but I had to bottle these emotions and keep this from John and lie to him. Well, he was so eager about the trip.

He was singing, laughing and couldn't sit still and would turn to me excitedly with eyes like dinner plates and a cheeky smile and say, 'I am going to catch the biggest fish, Kathy'. He was talking incessantly about all our fishing trips out the harbour, and all the fish he had caught, so passionate. Just couldn't stop talking about it.

I was staring out the window listening to John endlessly talk about his trips and periodically turning to look at him or answer a question all the while trying not to cry, for four hours. A long time to try and hide your emotions, however, John was so excited I don't think he even noticed my forlornness.

John was asking Dad repeatedly, 'When are we there?'

Dad would keep replying, 'Nearly their mate, not far.'

I would slouch deeper into my seat and stare further out the window watching the cane fields zoom by.

We started driving down this old dirt road and we came to these enormous black steel gates and brick walls running beside each gate. The words read out, "Townsville Bush Children's Home". John knew immediately where we were, even though he couldn't read or write, he knew. He was like a wild animal and his expression of excitement was replaced by absolute rage. He started punching the car windows and kicking the seats.

'You buddy bassards, I am not going in there,' he yelled.

Dad stopped the car and attempted to wrestle John and get him under control. At the same time Dad is yelling at me to go inside and get a Warden.

I ran in screaming, 'Help, Help, my Dad needs a hand with my brother, He has gone wild.'

Three Wardens came rushing out of the building with the big doors at the front flying open to assist Dad to hold John down. They were dressed in their white short-sleeve shirts and pants.

My Dad kept saying, 'He's a strong bugger. Watch out, he will kick and punch.'

They had a real struggle getting him under control and in the building literally dragging him kicking and screaming.

'You buddy bassards,' he yelled angrily.

I got back in the car and just slumped in my seat sobbing my heart out, and all I can remember is him screaming out. I couldn't even bring myself to look and I never had the chance to even say goodbye to John or give him a hug. When Dad finally came back out to the car, he was sweaty and breathing heavily, and took a moment to settle himself before getting into the driver's seat. I quickly straightened myself up, wiped away my tears and tried hard to stop crying. I was thinking I might be next and was going somewhere else too.

Kathy Howie

I said to Dad, 'Am I going back to Jonesy's now?'

He turned to me and said calmly, 'Oh yeah, love, it was only John going to a new home, because it was so hard for Rita to handle him.'

I was so upset but had to hold my anger, sadness, and fear in until I got back to Jonesy's, and back to some kind of safety. I didn't want to give Dad any reason whatsoever not to. It was going to be the longest drive home, but I think I was so exhausted and emotionally drained that I slept for most of it. I remember thinking John would hate me for life. Dad tried to console me and told me they will look after him well there and that he is better off in that place. I believe he was in there for about two years until he was sixteen. Once John had turned sixteen, Dad went up to Townsville to pick him up and bought him back to Mackay. I was so happy and excited that I would be reunited with my brother, however, apprehensive as he might not like me anymore or remember me. Dad found him a job in a workshop that repaired old lawn mowers and John seemed happy. I didn't see John much, only when I would go over to my sister's place sometimes for dinner or to play cards. John seemed to have put everything behind him, as he would always give me big kisses and hugs when he saw me. He hated my Dad for a long time, and was never too pleased to see him, greeting him with a scowl and silence.

8. School Days

I am still living at Jonesy's place, and enjoying school, my friends, and what family time I had. Dad got a new job and worked at the Mackay airport as a porter. I was so proud of him, because working at the airport was a very good job, and I would gloatingly tell all my friends at school. Whenever I was allowed, I would hurriedly ride my pushbike down to see him while he was working, excited to be able to hang out at the Airport.

I would wait for him patiently until he had a break, and he always gave me something for my glory box, or to put in my cubby house from one of the Airlines every time I visited him, which I accepted gleefully. Sometimes it was just a plate from Qantas, a cup from Ansett, or just a packet of chips. He just had to give me something.

He would say, 'What have I got for you today?'

I would say, 'I don't want anything Dad, I just came to see you.'

I wasn't used to getting many gifts, unless I had been made to earn it, and I don't know why he felt he had to give me stuff. Maybe it was guilt, or he was just trying to be the best dad he could. Funny Dad.

Back to school. Grade Seven. Being a catholic school, we were taught by Nuns, and our class had the worst Nun ever. Sister Mercury. Boy, did she love dishing out the punishment. Her cane became an extension of her right arm. Our school was a high set school, so we had to get to our classroom via stairs, and our classroom had fold out windows. I remember one day, Sister Mercury left the room, so Crystal decided to call out to our friend Josephine, who was down-stairs. I think we were getting up to some mischief in class and she was the lookout. So, she decided to hang half her body out the window looking for Josephine.

Crystal started yelling out, 'Is Sister down there?'

Josephine was yelling back, 'I can't see her.'

Next minute, Sister sneaks up the back stairs, quietly enters the classroom, grabs the cane off the blackboard on the way past, all the time watching us, and almost floating across the room. I am next to Crystal and had spotted Sister coming. I am nudging her to let her know of the imminent threat. I quickly ran back to my seat sitting as if I was oblivious to the whole situation. Crystal turned and saw Sister approaching with an evil eye. Crystal just froze and immediately knew her fate was sealed. Crystal copped it in front of the whole class, across the back of the legs, tears streaming down her face. Sister belted the hell out of her and just kept swinging endlessly, and it appeared as if she wasn't going to stop. Crystal was so sore, bloodied and bruised, and extremely embarrassed. I felt so sorry for Crystal, and somewhat guilty as I was her partner in crime. I used to be quite adept at maths and enjoyed it, as it came easy to me.

So, one day Sister decided to increase the pressure and said to the class, 'For every sum you get wrong you will get a caning.'

Here's a thought maybe reward and encourage students for getting them all right. Now I was generally a ten out of ten with maths, however, I was so terrified I got eight wrong, two out of ten. I just crumbled and I knew what was coming.

Sister said, 'Disgraceful, Kathleen, put your hands out palms facing up.'

I tentatively stretched out my hands, palms facing up urging my hands and body not to shake or pull my hands away. So, of course, I got eight times the cane across the palms of my hands. Hated that type of maths and obviously hated the pressure. My hands were so sore and bruised I couldn't even make a fist let alone hold the pencil, but I had to, or she would cane me again. Terribly sadistic, and sorry, but an evil twisted piece of shit. I am terribly sorry, Lord, for disrespecting your so called, chosen ones, but come on, this is why parents and teachers are not allowed to discipline children anymore. This wasn't punishment or discipline, it was abuse of children, which seemed to be the norm in those days. There's that saying again, "Children should be seen and not heard".

9. Good Times

There were many memorable and enjoyable times at Jonesy's, and it always gives me great comfort to recall these memories. She had lots of friends that would donate garbage bags full of clothes to me. I had so much fun rummaging through these big garbage bags of clothes. There were some absolutely gorgeous dresses. I would try on the items I liked, and put on a fashion show for Jonesy, and she would take a fleeting glance, looking up from her knitting, and either smile or shake her head. Maybe a comment like, "That's far too short." Or, "Your father wouldn't like that," or, "That colour doesn't suit you". For once in my life I felt like a princess, and I was the best dressed girl in town.

Jonesy was a good friend of the Manager of the local Woolworths store, and she often gave Jonesy all these broken chocolates that they couldn't sell. We would have dinner, which I would hurriedly scoff down, race through the dishes, and then we would sit and watch TV at night devouring chocolates, so yummy. I felt lucky to be living in my own Willy Wonka world. Jonesy knitted every night without fail, and I remember the click of the rapidly moving knitting needles. Sometimes I would see her watching the TV and still knitting not even looking at her progress. She would knit baby booties, baby nighties and baby bonnets and then pack them up in used men's shirt boxes. These boxes had a hard, clear plastic lid so she would present her creations in a way that people could see everything on display. It looked so pretty. She always sprinkled baby powder on them to make them smell nice. To this day I am not sure where, or who, she sold them to, but I am sure they were popular because she knitted every spare moment she had.

I had the most wonderful girlfriends I had always wished for as young child. The school we went to, was a girl's school, and all the girls were absolutely gorgeous and welcoming. My two besties were just amazing. Dana and Crystal.

One afternoon, after school, Crystal came over to my place to see if we could go somewhere. Crystal was always the ringleader and always had interesting suggestions of things to do. On this occasion, I wasn't allowed to go with them, although we could all stay and hang out at my place. This didn't appeal to us, so in our wisdom, we decided to sneakily climb out the window. Mind you, I am in a two-storey, or high set, house. Supporting the house are large wooden stumps with metal plates on top of each stump, which are known as Ant Caps. Crystal climbed out the window first, followed closely by me. Well her dress got caught on one of these ant caps on top of a post leaving her trapped halfway down, and me nowhere to go. I didn't want to go back in as I thought Jonesy might catch me, and we were on a mission of escape. Well, Crystal started laughing. I am thinking not so funny, however her laughter was infectious which caused me to laugh so hard, I lost all control and peed my pants. Subsequently the pee ran down my leg and all over Crystals head. Her laughter morphed into muffled screams and then back to laughter. We were laughing so much we couldn't move. Once we calmed down and regrouped, we climbed down and made the decision to venture quietly back upstairs to change my under-wear and Crystals clothes, but we got caught making a re-entry to the house.

Jonesy looked at us with a puzzled expression and said, 'I thought you girls were in your room.'

We were trying to contain our muffled giggles, not making eye contact with Jonesy, glancing at each other sideways, and quickly made our way back to my room, not daring to look back at Jonesy. We quickly shut the door, briefly glared at each other with wide eyes and burst into raucous laughter. We were like the Three Musketeers, mischievously running around the neighbourhood playing games and pestering neighbours. Normal kid stuff in those days.

On Friday nights, we used our entrepreneurial skills and collect, some might say steal, empty soft drink bottles from the neighbourhood. We would then ride our bikes down to the Caltex Service Station, bottles clinking in our baskets, and cash them in. We got five cents each for them and immediately spent our ill-gotten gains on lollies and chocolate. Sometimes, on the way to the Servo, we would ride down Pensioner Lane, and throw green guavas, which were rock hard, on their rooves. Crystal's dog, Goldie, would sometimes tag along, and she would run under their houses and scatter all the cats. All the time we are hiding, rolling around in laughter, not even contemplating how annoying we must have been. We would wake everyone up in Pensioner Lane, and probably thought it was hilarious.

We rode our pushbikes everywhere to beaches, shops, and our houses. we swam in dirty drains at the back of Crystal's house, climbed Crystal's Tamarind tree, and sat up there and ate so many tamarinds. Eating a lot of tamarinds, however, gives you a lot of gas and we would sit up there farting and giggling. We even turned that into a game and called it the twenty-one-gun salute.

I think around the same period of time, June rolled around, which meant the Mackay show was on. Dad let me know a few days earlier to dress up nice, and he would pick me up, take me to the show and we could go and have some fun. I was so excited and didn't sleep much the night before thinking of all the rides I would go on, and the show bags. *How am I going to carry them all?*

Dad was by no means a wealthy man, and rarely had two cents to rub together, so spending two dollars for anything was a big deal and was certainly a lot to get into the show back then. I desperately wanted a show bag of any kind but at a dollar each, Dad thought no way, highway robbery and full of cheap rubbish. He flatly refused to buy me a show bag. Dad justified his decision by saying he would take me down to the shop to buy a rubber, ruler, some pencils and a packet of chips, it would be far cheaper. For me though not the same as excitedly diving into that show bag and pulling out all the goodies.

Due to the cost of going to the show, he only took me once, and although I was disappointed leaving the show empty handed, I really treasured that time with him walking around holding his hand, eating Dagwood Dogs and looking at all the animals and rides. Even though, I never lived with him, he tried his best to be a good Dad, and be there for me. I needed that reassurance, I think.

Dad and I at my first and only Mackay Show

Although I had some wonderful and lovely times at Jonesy's, it wasn't always smooth sailing as it was with any teenager. At fourteen years old, it was the days of the mini-skirts, and I thought, *WOW they look fantastic.* I desperately wanted to have one, like all my friends. I was jointly refused by Jonesy and Dad, and not allowed to wear them. I had to be in boring old granny dresses that covered my knees. I was not happy at all and thought will I ever be able to make my own decisions. It's my life. Typical rebellious teenager.

October that year came around, and Dad had said school was a waste of time, and that I needed to get a job. I didn't even get to finish year Nine at school. I think it was more like, you are costing me too much money to go to school so get a job.

Dad came around to Jonesy's and told me get my best dress on, as he had arranged a job interview for me. Dad went to school with a gentleman I only knew as Mr. Berns. He owned a department store in Mackay called Bernie's. Once I had completed the interview, he hired me straight away and I started work the very next week. I don't know if this was irony or just cruel fate, but I was employed to work in the Men's clothing section. Of all places where I have to deal with men, measure them for size and be ogled at, however, I don't recall any issues there. Life just sucks sometimes.

After I had been working at Bernie's for close to a year, I decided to go upstairs to the Admin office. I was really curious about St. Nazareth Home, and what it was all about, as I had never been told or completely understood its purpose. I thought perhaps it was an orphanage, and maybe I had real parents out there somewhere. This is when I found out what sort of home it really was.

I asked the office girls politely if I could I use the phone, they said no worries, help yourself. I dialled the home and queried what sort of home this was. The person replied bluntly and without emotion, "It's a home for unwanted children". After a slight pause the person sharply said, "Is there anything else I can help you with, Madam?". I replied, "No thanks, that's fine." I then quickly hung up. I was just overcome with sadness and was doing everything to try and swallow the lump in my throat and stop from bursting into tears. 'UNWANTED' that word again I hadn't heard for so long.

I always thought that about the word, but to have it so bluntly, definitively, and coldly verified like that was still a shock. I was so angry, confused and upset. I also felt stupid contacting them in the first place, knowing all along what the answer would be, but secretly hoping it was something else. Perhaps a home for the gifted. *You Dickhead.* I still had a fair few hours to go before I finished my work, so I just tried to put on a happy face. I never ever told my Dad, or my Sister, about the phone call. I just tried to keep every horrible experience and dark moments in my life buried deep inside. Maybe this is why I am opening up now and speaking out and telling parents to be aware that their children will keep secrets when told to.

10. Freedom

Not long after that, I went to live with Dad's brother and his wife, Uncle Tom, and Aunty Sylvia. Uncle Tom had half an arm missing from an accident where his arm got caught and chewed up in a chaff cutter. They were lovely people, and I was only there for probably a year, with no issues or dramas until I told Aunty Sylvia, I had a boyfriend. Well she just flew into an uncontrollable rage, and just started punching me around the head. I never really found out why, but I knew right then and there, it was time to look after myself.

I have had enough of people thinking they can just abuse me or bash me whenever they liked. I decided to move into a lady's boarding house in Mackay. Cromer House. Small room, but all meals were included for seven dollars a week. Finally I had my own space, and freedom with no one telling me what to do, or where to go, or so I thought. The boarding house had some rules. Come on. Had to be in by ten pm every night, or you were locked out. I am guessing there was about thirty girls living there.

I met this gorgeous girl there, Narelle. We became good friends and used to hang around out on the veranda a lot and go to night clubs occasionally. Being a country girl, she was a bit shy at first, didn't go to the clubs as often as me. Just a lovely person. Then her sister moved into town to work at a bank. I was introduced to her by Narelle. Her name is Kerry and she was a bit more outgoing than Narelle, and wow, did we rock the town when we went out. Absolutely gorgeous sisters, and I became very close friends with Kerry, as we were of similar age. I really treasure lovely and friendly people. Kerry and I used to go out to the Shamrock, and have an absolute ball, drink, dance and just have fun. I have now known Kerry for forty-five years and she is helping me write this book. To this day we are still close friends, and even though we have both been living apart, and at times halfway around the world from each other or on opposite sides of Australia, we remained in contact and have a catch up as often as we could. I have been giving her a few OMG moments, and shocks whilst typing this book with me.

In the past I have only told Kerry small snippets of my life, and not the full story and horrible details. She can handle it though, she loves me, and we have been through a lot together and I am honoured to have her in my life.

Living on my own, earning my own money and paying my own bills sort of gave me a sense of really starting to grow up now, and have a life and mind of my own with no-one telling what to do, what to wear, and definitely no footsteps coming down the hallway to my door. I think Dad was also a bit relieved too, not having to pay my board and school fees anymore. As I reflect on this part of my life, I have had the sudden realisation that I just basically abandoned Jonesy, and that she would have really missed me.

I was just in such a hurry to get out on my own and live my own life, that I cannot ever remember going to see her or even wanting to go and see her anymore. Now I am older, I reminisce a lot about Jonesy, and dejectedly wish I had kept in contact with her. Jonesy was the closest person I had to a mother, and she taught me so many life skills I carry with me today. I honestly feel if she would have let me call her Mum that day, I asked her, it may have been different.

As I write this, it deeply upsets me that I never hugged her and said goodbye. I would have sincerely thanked her so much for looking after me, feeding me, clothing me, nurturing me, and teaching me how to be an independent woman. To this day it makes me feel terribly sad to think I was so unappreciative of her, and my selfishness and haste to be on my own cost me that opportunity. What I would really like to do one day is go and visit a medium, and hopefully I can get some messages to her of gratitude. "I love you Jonesy and always will".

Once I had moved out on my own, I even stopped hanging around with my two besties, Crystal and Dayna. They were still at school and I was working, living on my own, and going out all grown up. Perhaps I thought they were just school kids, and I was an adult; I don't know. It really saddens me that I didn't see those girls for thirty-three years. We have reconnected now, and have regular catch ups, and reminisce about the old days, and talk about our husbands and kids. Bloody stupid really, as they lived close to Cromer House. I can't explain why I just cut loving people out of my life so ruthlessly and without thought.

I think back now to my early life, and due to the fact that I was being shifted so many times, I was always making new friends and just as quick would lose them, never to see them again. I must have felt I had to start anew every time. Don't get too comfortable or close with people, as I would probably be moving on soon.

Occasionally Dad would drop in and visit me at Cromer House. We never had mobile phones or computers back then like we do nowadays. The only phone we had was downstairs, and when it rang someone nearby would answer it, and yell out to whoever it was for. Dad was living in a men's boarding house at the time, and the telephone situation was the same for him. I started going out every Saturday night, as I loved dancing, partying, and the freedom of doing what I want, like all teens then and now. Get paid Friday, pay rent, shopping Saturday morning, I would buy a new outfit for Saturday night. I would buy a new outfit every week. Spend the rest on the night out, broke by Monday, and back to work. Never saved any money at all. Back in those days I didn't care, though, as I was having too much fun. My money: I will do what I like with it.

11. First Love

I met my first boyfriend, Dick, at the age of sixteen and a half, he was eighteen and a half. I met him at the Shamrock. He was from Mt. Isa. We used to meet at the Shamrock every Saturday night. I was so, so, in love. He loved me so much but was a bit jealous at times. He would start fights with guys that would look at me too long or talk to me. A bit much, in a way, but I knew he really cared about me and it felt good to have someone to protect me. It didn't really help when I was wearing very revealing, sexy, and often very skimpy clothing and lots of miniskirts.

I remember the first time we got a little bit frisky, and he was trying to touch my boobs. Thoughts of my childhood days were flooding back. The mere thought of a man touching me in a sexual way made me apprehensive, and I got scared and pulled away and was saying, "Please don't", and I told him I was a virgin. He laughed at me. I felt like I had done something wrong and didn't really understand what a virgin really was. Or maybe I felt I was lying to him, as I had been touched in so many different ways as a child.

When I got home, I rang my friend to verify that I was a virgin.

She replied, 'Have you done it before?'

I said, 'No.'

My friend was not aware of my childhood history.

I asked her, 'Then why was he laughing.'

She said, 'At sixteen, it's a bit late to be a virgin.'

Men had never laughed at me, just sneered, and threatened me, so this was an unusual experience for me. For the next three months every time he tried to get intimate with me, I would come up with all sorts of excuses like headaches, not feeling well, and that I had my "monthly's". Eventually my excuses ran out, as did his patience, and I gave in to him and we made love.

I loved him and thought I would have lost him if I didn't succumb to his advances. It was of great comfort to me to have a man I loved, and that love was reciprocated, and there was also security to have someone to protect me. We were together for five years and, all in all, they were pretty good years, except for the last year. We were arguing and fighting constantly. One day he came to me and said he wanted to go home to Mt. Isa, and he asked me if I wanted to go with him. I said yes, I would like to start travelling again so, why not, and maybe our relationship might improve in a different environment.

Living In Fear Of Enemies

I think as a child, if you are in and out of homes and moving around so often, it seems to be embedded in you to keep moving, and can't wait to travel again, and go to a different place or home.

The first massive step was to get permission from my Dad to move up there. I don't know why, as I was an adult now, and didn't need people's permission to do things, but I respected and loved Dad too much to just leave him. After all, he is the only parent in my life, and I didn't want to lose him as well. Dad wanted to meet up with Dick's parents, who were staying in a caravan park on Harbour Road.

I hadn't even met them yet. My sister lived at the same caravan park. Dick's father was a preacher. Dad, my sister, and I went down and met Dick and his parents on a Saturday night. I had told my sister that his father is a preacher, so she told Dad not to take beer down or discuss politics. My Dad, what a legend. So, what does he decide to do? He decides to hide a six pack of XXXX behind his back and take it to the get together. He reckons I am not sitting down, and meeting someone without a beer in my hand, and I couldn't give a shit if he is a preacher. Then dad proceeds to bring up every possible political topic he could think of. This is just great. We felt so embarrassed. I couldn't look Dick's father in the eye. Having said all that, surprisingly the discussion went well, dad finished his six pack, and it was all organised that I could go to Mt. Isa and stay with Dick at his parent's house. Dad made it very clear that it was on the condition that I slept in a separate room. It was all so exciting to me.

12. Independence

We left for Mt Isa a few days later, and during the trip, we were travelling at night, we had a Min Min light follow us. They are balls of gas which look like a big spotlight or sun. It was following us along the side of the car. I was a bit scared, but Dick reassured me that it wasn't harmful. Finally, we arrived in Mt Isa. I followed Dad's rule most of the time, and we moved in with Dick's parents. I quickly got a job and about six months later we moved out into our own unit. Sorry, Dad, broke your rule.

One very hot and sunny day, six of us decided to clamber into one car and head out to Moondarah Dam. On the way Dick wanted to get some cigarettes, so we stopped at a hotel. Dick and I went inside and started talking to a friend who just happened to be in the hotel at the time. Apparently, we must have talked too long because when we went back outside the others had gone. They had just taken off and left us without saying a word. We had no other choice but to go back inside and have a few drinks in the hotel.

Well, we found out that afternoon, that our friends had hit this hill, which everyone calls the Thrill Hill, at an extremely high speed, ended up airborne and the car turned on its side and rolled about thirty times. Thankfully all our friends survived, but they were very badly injured. Heads hit, and went through windscreens, there were broken arms and legs, haematoma's to heads, and many bruises, and other broken bones.

They had been drinking and were all drunk at the time. I really think that if we had been in that car, we could have been worse off as we were the sober ones. One lucky escape for us. That was fate, we weren't meant to be in that accident. The car was a total write-off.

The very next time we tried to go out to Moondarah Dam, a car and a trailer were in front of us. All of a sudden, a tyre came off the trailer, bouncing down the road and sparks flew everywhere. This tyre was bouncing towards us, and when it was about thirty feet in front of us, we tried to dodge the tyre, but it hit the windscreen with a thud, and it felt like the car was going to crack in half. We swerved and ended up in a drain. Minor injuries and a bit of damage to the car. Moondarah Dam was the main place to go for daytime entertainment in Mt. Isa. Not very lucky for me on some occasions, but we did have some good trips out there. We had a friend with a speed boat, and we used to go water skiing with them.

Another popular past time in the Isa was roo (kangaroo) shooting. This particular time, we went out roo shooting just out of Mt Isa. We were in a little white ute, with a roll bar at the back mounted with spotlights. Roo shooting was always done on dusk and into the night. Dick and I were standing in the back of the ute on roo watch, with our spotlights scanning the night landscape for the bright eyes of kangaroos. I spotted this big red, he was huge. The signal to the driver when you spotted a roo was to bang on the roof of the ute. The driver would stop the ute, and the boys would grab their rifles, bound out of the ute, and get into position to shoot. On this occasion, I spot the big red. I bang hard on the roof of the ute several times with the palm of my hand, which hurt. The driver slammed on the brakes. However, I hadn't braced myself for the sudden stop and I went flying, hurtling over the roof and bonnet, landing on the dirt road about twenty feet in front of the ute. The boys flew out of the ute, rifles in hand, scanning the night landscape, primed to shoot.

Someone said, 'Who banged on the bloody roof?'

Dick said, 'Kathy did.'

Then everyone was going, "Where the hell is Kathy?". heads were swivelling looking for me. Meanwhile, I am out the front of the ute lying on the ground trying to speak, trying to yell out help, I was so winded and couldn't get a breath, no sound would come out. Finally, I think I might have uttered a groan and the boys found me battered and bruised and covered in red dust. By that time the Roo was gone, and I often imagine him bounding away laughing at me, middle finger proudly raised. We all laughed afterwards.

On another occasion, Dick's sister-in-law asked us to mind their prized show poodles, while they went away for a month. She adored these poodles and gave us some strict instructions. Everything was going well until, in our wisdom, we decided to take some advice from a friend, who told us that to make their ears real fluffy, you tie elastic bands around them, and leave them there for a week. Okay, sounds like a good idea. Disaster struck because the ears got infected, and one ear fell off one of the poodles. We decided to take them to the vet. He took one look at them, and said they had to be put down as the infection was too serious and couldn't be treated. Panic set in, as we couldn't afford to pay for the vet bill, so we did what we thought was the humane thing and took them out in the bush and shot them. I was trying to console the second dog as it was shaking furiously. At the same time Dick shot the first dog with a double-barrelled shot gun, however, I was far too close and got sprayed with blood from head to toe. I felt nauseous and overcome with sadness as we then had to shoot the second dog. Dick's sister-in-law wasn't due back for a week, so we had little time to ready ourselves for her return. On her return we explained what happened, and she went into a blind rage, and was furious, shaking, sobbing, and so upset. She absolutely hated us after that. She rarely spoke to us, never entrusted us to look after any possession of hers ever again. I wonder why ... oops. By the way, I love animals.

I had a lot of interesting and challenging experiences in the Isa. One of those was I got to drive a Big Mac truck road train, with two trailers, from Mt. Isa to Mary Kathleen. So awesome, but terrifying at the same time. A friend of ours owned it and asked me to go on a trip with him. He encouraged me to get in the driver's seat, and I looked at the dash and there were buttons and dials everywhere. I then grabbed the gear stick, and my friend explained that the truck had 32 gears and 5 reverse. My brain is just having a seizure trying to comprehend that. He decided to challenge me and make me drive through this caravan park. I was shitting myself, and not too happy about it but hey, let's have go. I was knocking out tent pegs, ropes and dragging tents. I was trying not to hit any, but I think I got them all. I pulled up and got out of the driver's seat, it was just too intimidating. Peter took over until we were back out on the main road, and then I took over again back to Mt. Isa. On the open road I absolutely loved it, and got accustomed to the gears, and all the machinations of driving a road train. An experience I look back on proudly.

Dick, his brother, Dan, and I, once did a trip from Mt. Isa to Chincilla, some fifteen hundred kilometres away. We were going to pick up a Bedford truck for Dick's father. We would drive a car there, leave the car in Chinchilla, pick up the Bedford truck, and drive back to Mt. Isa. This Bedford truck had strong arm steering, which is effectively no power steering, no air conditioning, and rode as rough as guts. So, there was Dick, Dan, and me, humming along in this truck. We did have a fun trip. Dick did most of the driving, but I drove some of the way. Dan was too young to drive. We decided to pull into this pub somewhere in outback QLD for a few beers. It was one of those pubs, where everythign went silent, and all the locals stared at you with piercing gazes when you walked in. Because we felt so popular, NOT, we decided to lie and say we were from a band.

It didn't even cross our minds that they might ask us to sing. Anyway, that changed everything. I was the singer, of course, Dan was the drummer, and Dick was the guitarist. I don't know what the band's name was though. They all believed our bullshit and even more importantly we were shouted drinks. We left the hotel very merry and a bit wobbly. Dan being younger and under-age was just being a pestering drunk, so we told him to sit on the back of the open tray. Off we go with Dan on the tray, however, he was so drunk he kept falling off the back of the truck, and onto the dirt road. He was bleeding everywhere, and covered with red dust. We cleaned him up a bit, and Dick and I decided to leave him on the tray. This time we restrained him and tied one arm and one leg to the frame of the truck behind the cabin. I am not sure how long it was, but he slept for hours.

We threw a fan belt and broke down about twenty kilometres from Mt. Isa. We were stuck on the side of the road for hours. Not many cars out that way. An elderly couple driving towards us pulled over, and we explained our issues.

The little old lady said, 'I can fix that.'

We were looking at her like she was some old woman with dementia.

She said, 'Hang on, I have a pair of stockings in my port.'

We looked at each other perplexed and thought what the hell is she going to do with that. She tied them around the two fan belt wheels, and to our amazement, the engine fired up, and we made it back to Mt. Isa. God love her. We were out in the middle of nowhere. It is like a desert out there.

Mt. Isa became a place where I could ignore my past for a while and put all those bad memories behind me. I didn't think much about my friends back in Mackay, my dad, or my sister. I think I had moved on with my life and was living life my way. Dad would ring occasionally to see how I was. I had gotten to the stage where I no longer cared about my mother, or even registered that she existed. I wasn't interested in seeing her, talking to her, or hearing from her. She was just a fleeting dream, or perhaps a nightmare. I am still in Mt Isa minding my own business and enjoying life.

13. The So-Called Mother

One day, in 1975, out of the blue, my sister rang me and advised me that my mother was dying of a tumour in the stomach. I didn't really give a rat's arse, to be honest, *"so what,"* I thought, *"she deserves it"*. Apparently, my mother was living in Maryborough with some boyfriend at the time. *"Good,"* I thought, *"the further away the better"*. My sister demanded that I come down from Mt. Isa on the train, meet up with her at the Mackay train station, and we would then travel together to Maryborough to see her. Great, I really didn't want to go. I felt it was a waste of time and money. Something hit me, and there was this lingering thought and overwhelming curiosity to see what she looked like. Maybe she's regretful for her choices, and maybe she might answer a few questions. She, at least, owes me that. So, off I go, boarded the train down to Mackay, and met with my sister at the station. No hugs, kisses or emotions, and it was a cold reunion. I can't recall if we talked much on the trip to Maryborough. We pulled into the station at Maryborough, and the train jolted to a stop.

I looked out the window and said to my sister. 'There is only an old couple waiting there.'

I immediately thought, *typical mother can't even turn up to greet us.*

My sister looked out the window, and said excitedly, 'Oh that's her.'

My limited memories of my Mother were of this beautiful young woman. I could never work out how my sister knew her, as I thought Mother had abandoned us all. Maybe she had kept in contact with her and had been seeing her over the last few years. The greeting was extremely awkward. I didn't know what to say, or where to look, and there were no joyous smiles, or rushing into each other's arms. I don't even know if I cuddled her. I suppose I did. Hang on a minute, she is supposed to be dying of a stomach tumour. Why was she here and not in hospital, how is she supposed to be dying? In retrospect, I think it was just a ploy to get me there. That was mother's *modus operandi*, in my experience with her. She never explained why she didn't want to see me before. Stupid bloody woman. We went out to the pub for tea that night. Everything seemed fine. We had okay conversation, still a very distant, and cold vibe lingered. I didn't dare bring anything up from the past, as I didn't want to ruffle too many feathers just yet or scare her off. I remember thinking, *"maybe there is chance we could reconnect"*. The next morning, I was quietly doing the dishes after breakfast, and the mother came out of the bedroom in her dressing gown, lighting up a smoke, and demanded that I drive her car down to the bottle shop to get her a bottle of OP Rum. I didn't have a licence at this stage.

I said, 'No problem, I will do it in a minute,' so that I could finish the dishes.

She stormed out of the kitchen back to her room and within a couple of minutes she came storming back out of the bedroom, slammed her hand on the table, so loud and yelled, 'I told you to get my rum.'

I was so humiliated, and embarrassed, and to think she has never been any sort of mother, and now she is trying to tell me what to do. Where was she when I needed discipline, guidance, and love as a child? Now I am a rebellious teenager, you think I am going to be at your beck and call. It really got my back up, and it infuriated me.

I said, 'Alright, I'll go get your rum.'

I went down to the pub, got her bloody OP Rum, and threw it on the kitchen table, packed my bags, and I was on the next train out of there back to Mt. Isa.

My sister was mad with me and yelled at me, 'But she's your mother. She's your mother.'

I just walked out and ignored her and didn't even acknowledge the Mother. She was most likely drowning in her rum. I don't know why my sister was like that, she knew she wasn't a mother and especially never been one to me. Despised them both.

14. More Abuse

I returned to Mt Isa angry, hurt, and, once again, rejected. At one point, Dick and I had a huge argument because I was talking to some guys I knew from Mackay, who were now living in Mt. Isa. He was furious, and said I looked like a slut, amongst other names. This just flooded my mind with memories of when I was a child in that house, being molested, and getting discovered by the wife, and that bitch telling me to get out of her house, and being called a dirty little slut. So, I didn't take that too kindly, and decided to leave him. I went back to Mackay for two weeks and stopped with my sister. What the bloody hell for, I don't know. I didn't really have anywhere else to go, I guess. I didn't even try to look up my old school friends or Kerry. Maybe I was embarrassed, it had been a few years. This was one of many times that I left him. However, unfortunately and stupidly, I did keep going back. Dad was furious, and unforgiving, when I kept going back to him.

Dick got a transfer from Mt Isa to Hervey Bay with his work, and I, of course tagged along. Everything was fine for a little while, then one night he got really intoxicated. We went home, I don't know what we were arguing about, but he threw me on the bed and started punching me wildly all over the body. I was screaming at him and pleading him to stop. Apparently the landlord, who lived upstairs above us, heard the commotion and screams.

The next day, Bob, the apparent boyfriend that was living with my mother in Maryborough, which is twenty minutes from Hervey Bay, had rung the landlord to talk to me about the vacuum cleaner I had borrowed off him. Which is really weird, because I don't remember how I ended up with the vacuum cleaner. Just a random memory.

The landlord decided to tell him there had been some screams and a lot of commotion coming from downstairs in our apartment. Bob then rang my Dad and told him all about what happened. Well, Dad rang the landlord and asked to speak to me. He was not happy at all and disgusted with me. Told me to get my arse back home. I did what dad asked and went home for a short time. Dick got a job with a company on the oil rigs and had moved to Adelaide. He contacted me and asked me to go to Adelaide with him, and that he had changed. I realised he had been getting increasingly abusive. I chatted with Dad about it and he told me never to go back with him. Idiotically I disregarded dad's advice, and I went back to him and lived with him in Adelaide. We resided in Glenelg, a little beach suburb, and I really enjoyed my time there. After a few months, he then got a transfer with the oil rig company to Sale in Victoria. Hey, haven't been there before, so off I go to Victoria. Getting to do a bit of travel as well. After six months, we split up once again, and I went back to Mackay.

Again I stayed with my sister and her husband. I just keep putting myself in shitty situations, and was becoming a pattern, but had nowhere else to go. Dad was furious and disowned me. I had visited him in the pub.

He looked at me and said, 'I am in better company here.'

He then turned back to his pot of beer and ignored me. I walked out of that pub, feeling as if I had let my Dad down, and that I had lost him forever. Who do I turn to now for any sort of family support?

I had terrible bunions on my feet, so while in Mackay, I decided to get my bunions operated on. I was going to do one at a time. I had the first one done, and was in excruciating pain, and hobbling around on crutches. I was laying in my room, and my sister and her husband had a massive fight one night. The next day my sister decided to get out of town, and left on the train to go down south, I assume to Mother's. I was left there with my brother-in-law and feeling vulnerable and alone. I didn't have a car, and I had to rely on other people to get me around, and I was still on crutches. My brother-in-law decided to get drunk one night while Sarah was away, and started trying to muck around with me, sexually. I was terrified, incapacitated, and practically at his mercy. I couldn't even run out the door. I felt trapped. I had no car and on crutches, so I rang a friend up, and asked her to come and pick me up. She came around immediately and rescued me. Problem was she lived in a caravan, and I lived with her for a while.

It was a struggle though, trying to get myself in and out of the caravan, and the trip to the showers was quite an effort on crutches. Also holding my shower bag between my teeth and juggling, make up, towel and clothes. A couple of days later, I had Dick on the phone begging me to go back to him. He sounded remorseful and expressed that he was missing me. *Don't do it, you idiot,* I thought, however, I still had some feelings for Dick, and didn't have too many other options at that time. I decided, once again, to go back to him.

15. Victoria

Dick was living in Sale at the time, which is in Gippsland, in the South Eastern part of Victoria. I was not game to let Dad know that I was, once again, going back to Dick, but he found out anyway, from my sister Sarah. Bitch, she hated me. Suffice to say, Dad didn't see me off. I think he had given up on me. With not much money, I asked around to see if anyone was heading down south. My girlfriend Kerry said she knew of a couple of guys heading to Sydney. They had a panel pan more commonly known as a Sin Bin or Shaggin' Wagon. They were happy to take me with them. I was appreciative, but a bit scared to start off with as I didn't know them at all. I assumed Kerry wouldn't send me any dubious characters.

It worked out that they were really lovely guys and treated me with respect. How refreshing. I lay in the back of the van and slept most of the way, as I was still on crutches recovering from my bunion operation. They would ask politely if I wanted anything to eat or drink and got it for me. They drove straight through and didn't stop anywhere other than to get fuel or food.

Kathy Howie

It took a day and a half, and I gave them some money for petrol. That took the pressure off them money-wise as well. They dropped me off at the railway station in Sydney, and I went from there to Melbourne. It was extremely daunting for a country girl from Mackay, QLD, pulling into the railway station at Melbourne; I felt a little nervous and disorientated.

When I hopped off the train, I proceeded to the luggage window to collect my port.

I asked the guy there, 'Can you tell me where the ports are?'

He started explaining to me, very helpfully I might add, that I had to catch a tram, and a bus to the ports, and pointed where the tram stop was. It was bitterly cold, and I was panicking, thinking how I am going to get there to collect my port.

A very nice lady that I had been sitting with on the train, saw my dilemma and came up to me and said, 'Are you alright?'

Frantically I said, 'No, they must have dropped the ports off five stations before we got here.'

She said, 'Are you talking about your suitcase?'

She explained that you have to say suitcase in Victoria, not port. He was sending me to the Port of Melbourne! Not funny mate! I absolutely hated Melbourne when I first turned up. I didn't realise how cold it could get down there. I had this little pink dress on, struggling with my crutches and suitcase.

People madly rushing around everywhere, as if they had to be somewhere right now. I didn't have a jumper or a jacket, so I had to find a shop to buy a jumper. I had to pay eighty dollars, because apparently, in the city of Melbourne, there are no cheap stores, only Myers and David Jones, and other shops of that calibre. I then ducked and weaved my way back to the railway station, on my crutches mind you, to catch another train to Sale. It took about three hours to get to Sale. Sale was even colder. *What am I doing?*

I met back up with Dick, and he seemed excited, and lovingly happy to see me. Love is blind at the age of twenty, and you tend to gloss over indiscretions. He took me to his unit, and suddenly confessed to me that he did have a girlfriend in Sale however, he had split up from her the day before. How convenient. That very first night I slept there, the ex-girlfriend came around banging on the windows, yelling and screaming. She had a girlfriend with her as back up, and they pinched the hose. Dick ran outside, yelling at them to go away. I realised then I was going to have a bit of trouble from this girl. Once again, I thought, *you Idiot what are you doing here?* Dick and I were together for about a year, and then the fights started all over again, and we were back to square one.

One day I proclaimed that I was going to get my hair cut.

He said, 'If you do, I will leave you.'

Not thinking that he really meant it, and most likely out of spite, I got it cut. My hair used to be down to my waist, now it's like a boy's haircut. He was pissed off to say the least. We struggled along, and within about a month, he said he had a wedding to attend in Mt. Isa.

I took him to the airport, and as we were kissing and cuddling goodbye, he started sobbing. He was waving back to me as he got on the plane, whilst balling his eyes out. I thought to myself, he is not coming back.

I was dead right.

That asshole ghosted me. I tried numerous times to contact him, and he just ignored all my phone calls and messages.

I wrote this poem about one sided love knowing he wasn't coming back.

One Sided Love

You can love someone with all you heart,
And put them on a throne.
But if they do not love you back,
You're better off alone.

There is a saying I once heard,
A real long time ago.
One that has stuck in my head,
And to this day I will know.

This I will share with you,
But please do not despair,
There is someone out there,
That does really care.

Do not walk in front of me,
I may not follow.
Do not walk behind me,
I may not lead.
Just walk beside me.

So, when you find that someone,
Walking beside you and being your friend,
This will take away the hurt,
And then you heart can mend.

Kathleen Howie

Here I was stuck in Sale, with no friends or family, no money and all alone. I decided to ring Dad, knowing he wasn't happy with me, but hey, I am his daughter, and he will understand. Dad didn't want a bar of me.

He dismissively said, 'No daughter of mine is so stupid to go back and forth in an abusive relationship.'

He said he would never talk to me again. Don't contact me again he said angrily. The one person I thought I could rely on has disowned me. I just slumped down onto the floor defeated, ashamed and abandoned.

I started to spiral into a deep depression.

16. Drugs and Depression

My life in Sale was an experience that was nothing to be proud of. It was one of the lowest points of my life. While I was with Dick, he never let me have any friends, and he was so jealous of me when I was working behind the bar, known as the Oil Pub. So, I had to start all over again. No friends, no money, and no toys again.

Not long after Dick left for Mt Isa, I had the police on my doorstep. There was a loud knock at the door. They asked me my name, my mother's name, which I wasn't really sure of, to be perfectly honest, as I never had a need to know it. I wasn't sure on her last name or maiden name. Asked me my father's name. I think to make sure they had the right person.

'Okay then, ma'am, we need to go inside, and we need you to sit down,' said one of the officers.

My immediate thought was something had happened to Dad. I sat down apprehensively.

The Police said, 'Your mother has died in a car

accident in Ceduna, South Australia. She was travelling from Adelaide to Perth. She was driving in the car by herself.'

My initial response to the police was, 'Oh my God, thank God for that.'

My reaction was not what they expected, and they looked at each other puzzled and looked back at me strangely.

They said, 'That was easy. Are you not concerned or upset?'

I said, 'I didn't know my mother that well, and I was really worried that you were going to tell me that my dad had passed away.'

The police finished up there visit with a few more questions, and promptly left. After the police had left, I actually slumped down on the chair, and started crying, not because I missed her, but I needed answers. All these thoughts were racing through my head. *Why did you abandon me? Why did you leave me at those awful places? Was I not good enough to be your daughter?* The sudden realization hit me like a hammer, that I am never going to get answers from her anymore on why she left me. What's gone is gone. No answers.

When I went to work, my boss offered to pay for me to go to the funeral. I said I am not interested in going to the funeral. Everyone believed that everyone has this wonderful mother in their life, that they treasure, trust and love. I never had that, ever, and people can't understand that, and why I feel the way I do. They don't know my history, and how my mother had treated me, and I am not about to explain it to them now, or really even want to. Let the past be in the past I thought.

Within two days of her death, I had her sister, Aunty Phyllis, contact me asking if I could contribute some money towards the funeral. The nerve of them to even ask me. Well, did I let her have it.

I said, 'No! You have got to be joking. I'm not putting money in for her. She can be chucked in the gutter for all I care, that's where she basically left me. She let me go with one pair of shoes for four years, and anyway, I don't even know you to send you any money.'

I hung up in her ear. I could have said one of a thousand things like; "She abandoned me", or, "She dumped me at a home for the unwanted", however, I was more upset about the shoes. It was only later on, when I was going over the call in my head that it suddenly dawned on me; it was her sister's husband, George, who was one of the guys molesting me when I was a child. Made me sick. How dare they.

So, here I was stuck in Sale, East Gippsland area of Victoria, and it was all foreign to me. My so-called boyfriend has gone, never to return. My father has disowned me. I did have a person who I considered a friend, Brenda. Brenda felt sorry for me after my boyfriend had left me. I couldn't afford to pay the rent on the unit by myself and would soon be homeless. I couldn't even afford to buy a train or plane ticket home to Mackay. Brenda asked me if I would like to go home with her, and meet her mum, Donna, and maybe stay there for a while. Brenda, her Mum, and her siblings lived in Maffra, a little country town just out of Sale. This was where I met her mum, and her sister Carol. When I met Brenda's mum, I was quietly surprised to see that she was an Aboriginal woman. Brenda never mentioned her mum was an aboriginal woman. Brenda had very blonde hair, very pale skin and blue eyes so there was nothing about her that indicated she was of aboriginal decent, and it didn't even cross my mind to ask.

I eventually got Brenda on her own and asked her if that is her real Mum.

She said, 'Yes. I am part Aboriginal. My father was of Caucasian decent, but not sure what nationality.'

Her sister, Carol, also had fair skin, but went very brown if tanned. I lived there for a few weeks, and eventually we all moved into Sale. I am not sure why we moved, but Maffra was absolutely freezing, so was Sale for that matter. Brenda had ten siblings; such a huge family, and fun to be a part of, but something I was unfamiliar with.

One died at the age of two as a result of a drowning. She was a twin and the exact same age as me, and her birth date was exactly the same as mine. It was extremely eerie and somewhat of a coincidence and seemed like it was fate that I became friends with Brenda, the other twin. It was especially evident to Brenda's mum, as she felt God had given back her daughter, in me. Same age, same birthdate, and a girl. So, Brenda's mum sort of unofficially adopted me, and I became a member of the family for a long time. Made me feel extremely good, loved and wanted for the first time in my life. Finally, I had found a little family. Donna took me in and treated me as if I was one of her own.

I got a job in Sale, in a pub that Brenda worked at. This worked out well back in Maffra, as we drove in together every day and became closer. It was about a twenty-minute drive. That was when Donna decided that we would move into Sale. Everything was going very well, and life was good for a while.

I started to develop this nervous condition. I would go out to discos and nightclubs dancing, I would be having a really good time, and then this strange feeling would wash over me, and I would start trembling, feeling nervous and uncomfortable. I was just trembling inside, and I couldn't understand what triggered it or even why it was happening. I decided to make an appointment and see the Doctor and, as was the standard practice back then with mental issues, lets prescribe some medication, so he put me on Serepax, a drug used to treat anxiety. At the time I trusted the doctors and followed their advice. I discovered later they were nerve tablets. They were working really well, and seemed to keep my condition under control, however, I don't think you are supposed to drink with this type of medication, but of course I did.

I was young and in party mode and really didn't care. The medication seemed to calm me down, and I felt they were doing a fantastic job. They also seemed to curb the overwhelming feelings of loneliness and abandonment. Even though I had been accepted by this wonderful family in Sale, it still felt as though I was an outcast. In fact, they were awesome tablets, and I began to rely on them to function on a daily basis. I began by taking the prescribed amount of three per day. After a while I started taking six per day, instead of the prescribed three. Two in the morning, two at lunch and two at night. One particular night, I took excessive amounts of Serepax, and drinking straight Scotch, and beer chasers. Not sure what the occasion was. I was just spiralling out of control. I kept going up to the kitchen in the pub where I worked asking for Brenda. Apparently about ten times, and they told me she had gone home hours ago. The next day Brenda's boss had told her I was absolutely crazy, and out of my mind.

I believed at the time the Serepax just seemed to make life a bit easier and removed all the pain. The tablets just made me so relaxed. I just didn't care, I would go to work, head home and pop more pills. They seemed to fix everything. In the end my boss cut my hours right down to almost nothing and then he put me off. I then had no options and ended up on the dole (unemployment). I look back now and realize, I was just turning up to work under the influence of the Serepax in the end, however, I had become increasingly more reliant on them. To get more tablets I would go to three different Doctors and then three different Chemists. When you become addicted you become desperate.

I am glad to see that is much more difficult to do that these days. I was an absolute mess. It was awful. I think back now, and it shocks me at how out of control I was. I was just lost and felt I had no-one to turn to, and that's when you continue to spiral.

On another night I left the nightclub early. I bought a bottle of Stones Green Ginger Wine and took it to a nearby park. I just sat there on the park bench, all by myself in the pitch black of night. I proceeded to drink the whole bottle. I was in a deeply depressed and vulnerable situation. Feeling all alone, thinking to myself, I've got no mother, I've got no father, I've got no boyfriend. No-one loves me or wants me. There was a fine line you walk when you suffer with depression. I was creeping ever closer to that line. Thoughts of suicide entered my mind. I didn't care about anyone. I didn't care about myself. Sick of life and how cruel it was. What's the point, no-one will miss me anyway? I managed to gather my thoughts enough to make my way home and pass out, perhaps hoping I wouldn't wake up.

I did meet this lovely girl, Katie, and she had overdosed on heroin years before I met her. She was on a lot of antidepressants to bring her off the heroin addiction. I went around to her place, she lived with her father. Her father warned me to be careful, as she gets a bit of schizophrenia, so if anything happened with her, I had to ring him, and he would be there in seconds.

Katie and I knocked around together for about six months, and one day we happened to be up town, about nine am. She started clapping her hands, out of the blue, trying to wake everyone up. She envisioned everyone around her was asleep. She was yelling at the top of her voice, "WAKE UP, WAKE UP, everybody get out of bed you lazy shits". I was freaking out. I had to run to the nearest phone box and ring her father. Next minute, he arrived, as does the ambulance, which I thought was a bit extreme. Apparently, she had not been taking the medication she was supposed to be taking. I had to leave her with her father and Ambo's. I just went home, and go through in my mind, what I had just experienced.

Katie ended up in Royal Park Psychiatric Hospital. A couple of weeks later I decided to catch the train down to Melbourne, and then a tram out to Royal Park to visit her. I approached this rather large red bricked building with cream trim and green posts supporting the veranda roof. It was surrounded by a wire fence, with a small gate for an entrance. There was no security or any guards, so I just walked through the little gate at the front, ignorant of any dangers. The lawns and gardens were well maintained, and it didn't appear threatening until I saw the bars on the windows. Suddenly, this guy came from nowhere and just started chasing me yelling, "I come home with you, I come home with you".

It was then that a bit of fear crept in. I started freaking out and I was terrified as this point. I rapidly made my way to some sort of reception which was positioned just inside the front door. I advised them that I was here to visit Katie. I was then advised to have a seat, and after some time, I was finally able to see Katie, and was escorted to her room. She was very docile and appeared to be heavily sedated, giving me single word answers, as if I wasn't even there. She seemed to be staring into the darkness of her own mind. I was still heavily reliant on my Serepax. Maybe that explained why there was no initial fear walking into a mental hospital. We chatted for quite a while and I kept her to date with the comings and goings of Sale.

I looked across at the other bed across from her, and there was a lady with shiny, silvery blue lips.

I asked Katie, 'What is that lady wearing on her

lips.'

Katie said, 'She is so stupid, she is wearing nail polish on her lips and lipstick on her nails.'

I had to use every bit of self-control not to laugh. I endeavoured to be positive and told Katie she was going to come good and get out of there soon. It was not a nice place to be in at all. I left after some time, and as I walked through the main doors, I began crying because I had to leave Katie there, and that guy started chasing me again. All the way to the gate. He just wanted to get out of there. I immediately thought I never ever want to go into a facility like that as a patient. What a hell hole. They had bars on the windows, like a prison. Wardens and Nurses were running around everywhere in a constant state of readiness like they were looking after criminals and expecting a riot or escape any minute. I sobbed for a long way back to Sale until the gentle rocking of the train and clickety clack of the wheels hypnotised me to sleep.

John, a customer at the pub I worked at, asked me out on a date, and we went out to a nightclub to dance and party. He had been invited to a party and it was at Dick's ex-girlfriend's place. I told him I couldn't go, for obvious reasons, however, he was relentless, and he talked me into going. We got to the door and Dick's ex-girlfriend, Rita, said scornfully "Kathy you are not allowed into this party and John said, "It's OK she is with me, so she is invited and my guest". Rita stubbornly agreed, and we both walked in and all was okay for a while. I noticed Rita kept walking in and out of this room with different boys, one after the other, and all the girls at the party were telling me that she has sex with anyone. After a while I was getting a bit irate with this behaviour.

One time when she came out of the bedroom, I said, 'You are a bit of a whore, Rita.'

She turned to me and said, 'You are nothing but a slut yourself.'

I thought to myself, *no one calls me a slut*. This comment made me regress to when I was called a slut as a little girl by Mrs Gordon. An intense and blind rage came over me, and I ferociously grabbed her by the hair and threw her into the bedroom. Then I threw her onto the floor and put my foot on her throat. I was telling her to say sorry. Over and over, I kept screaming at her to say sorry. Violent thoughts went through my mind and I wanted to smash the stubby I was holding in my hand, break it, and shove it into her neck. I guess I can thank God for helping me in that moment. I swung wildly with the stubby in my hand and hit her across her cheekbone with the stubby still in one piece. I stormed out the door and slammed it shut. The door then burst open and she had produced a rifle from under the bed. She came out with looks to kill and advanced towards me with the rifle raised.

She poked the rifle in my face and screamed. 'You bitch, I am going to bloody shoot you.'

I quickly turned and bolted for the front door, never looking back waiting for the bang, and took off running down the street. I left my date John there. I just kept running and running back into town never once looking back. I ended up at my park bench again. No alcohol this time. I just sat in the park, to gather my breath and thoughts for about an hour and then went home. John apparently had already been around home looking for me. He was mad with me for leaving as it embarrassed him. *How does that work?* So that was the end of that brief relationship. I ditched that bloke really quickly. Never saw him again. Never wanted to. All this time I am full of Serepax and alcohol. Never had a clear mind, and not thinking straight. Dark clouds around me all the time and no light to find a way out.

The next day I found out that she had gone to the Police Station in the morning to put me up for assault. The police said it is too late to report now, and that she should have done it the night before, when it happened. Thank God. I found out two days later that I had ruptured her Optic nerve in her eye, and she now had to wear glasses for the rest of her life.

At the time, I was so out of it on Serepax and alcohol, I didn't care about myself, I didn't care about anybody else, I didn't care about anything. I just didn't care, now in my middle age years, and where my life is now, looking back, it makes me cringe. I guess I dodged a bullet there, well really, I dodged two bullets, potentially.

I never was, nor ever have been, a violent person when I am clear headed and in control of my thoughts. To this day it makes me shiver to think that I even hit anybody like that or behaved in that manner.

I decided to go for a little holiday up to Orbost with Carol at Donna's sister's place. Orbost is in the North eastern part of Victoria, and it gets extremely cold there and often snow falls. Snow was falling on this occasion. This was the first time I had seen snow after all those years I thought I would see snow in Mackay.

Before I go any further, I need to explain that the bunionectomy I had done in Mackay, was not successful. The operation performed back then had caused my toe to collapse. I saw a doctor in Melbourne, and he had put in a screw and a Kirschner wire to straighten my toe back.

Now back to the little holiday. It was freezing cold on this particular night in Orbost. We were sitting by a huge log fire inside. I was so cold; I was sitting closest to the fire and I had my feet resting near the edge of the fire to keep my toes warm. We were having a few drinks. I had probably taken Serepax as well. I hadn't noticed my foot had been leaning on a log and had melted the bottom of my shoe.

Well, I suddenly jumped up in pain with the realisation that the fire had slowly heated up the Kirschner wire in my toe, which was made of stainless steel and it was burning the hell out of my foot. My foot was burning from the inside. I was running around yelling and screaming at the top of my voice, I ran out the front door, flinging my shoes off in mid stride and jumped in the snow to try and cool my foot down.

As you may or may not be aware, stainless steel doesn't cool down very quickly. I had my foot near the heated log so long it melted my shoe. I realised I had to get this Kirschner wire out of my foot sooner rather than later. This can only be done once everything is healed, so no more close proximity to fires. I left Orbost, after my short stay, and headed back to Sale for a couple of days. I booked an appointment with a doctor in Melbourne, and then went down there to eventually have the wire removed. While I was in Melbourne, Katie was simultaneously being released from Royal Park Mental institution. I got in touch with her, and we decided to meet at Flinders Street Station, the meeting place of Melbourne in the city, and she came back with me on the train. I was so happy that I had my beautiful friend back, and she appeared to be as normal as ever. It just felt so wonderful. Loved her.

Back in Sale everything was fine for a while, well what I perceived was fine. I met this nice girl named Nikki. She got into the Serepax as well and joined in with me taking them. She ended up buying some from me as well, as I could get them much more easily. We were soon having drug and alcohol fuelled sessions on a regular basis, sometimes daily. I guess she wasn't really a friend and realised she was using me, but we had something in common. One afternoon, around four pm I think, I was in my drug induced stupor, and so depressed that I decided I would lay down. Staring at the ceiling I turned my head and looked at my tablets on the side table, and I saw I had about a third of a bottle of my Serepax left. I went out into the kitchen and got a large glass of water and told Donna I am just going to lay down for a bit. I got into the bedroom, grabbed my tablets, and thought, *I am going to take the lot, if I die, I die, if I don't, I don't. I didn't' really care anymore.*

I can even remember thinking that there was enough there to overdose me. I just didn't care. I just wish they were sleeping tablets, where I could just go to sleep, and I know I would never wake up and die from them. Being nerve tablets, I didn't know what was going to happen. Still didn't care. I took them all, one at a time; just pop the tablet and wash down. I think there was about thirty. I laid down, shut my eyes and just went to sleep. I thought this is so peaceful, this is so lovely this is the best way to go. Next minute, Katie entered the bedroom and quickly assessed the scene, and started to violently shake me and wake me up.

I said to her in a soft, slurred and drug induced voice, 'Go away.' I put my finger up to my mouth and went, 'Sssshhhh.'

Without saying anything, I glanced over at my empty Serepax bottle. She looked at it and then looked back at me.

With absolute shock and horror on her face, she said, 'You didn't.'

I kept putting my finger over my mouth and going, 'Ssssshhhh.'

I just wanted to be left alone and go to sleep, wherever that led me to. I heard her running out of the bedroom and faintly yelling out to Donna saying I had overdosed. I could hear them come into the bedroom, they grabbed me and attempted to drag me out of bed. I could hardly walk I was like jelly and I didn't really want to help them anyway. They shoved me in the car and raced me off to the hospital.

When we got there, they both grabbed an arm, again

attempting to drag me out. This time I was little more aware and started to dig my heels in so they couldn't move me, refusing to get out of the car. I kept saying I want to go home, leave me alone. They eventually got me in the hospital emergency and the doctors gave me this black liquid, and what it is, I have no idea. They put a tube down the back of my throat and pumped the black liquid into me. Next minute I was convulsing and vomiting my guts out. I was so sick. My blood pressure then dropped dangerously low. All the nurses and Doctors were running around like crazy. They gave me an injection of something. I don't know what it was, but it immediately brought my blood pressure back up to normal.

The next day I woke up in a haze and confused about where I was. I had tubes running out of me. I didn't understand why at the time. I remember going to the day room just to get out of my ward and move around a bit. A nurse came around and did the observations on everyone. She checked my blood pressure and was concerned it had dropped very low again and I was starting to feel really sick. She quickly put me in a wheelchair and took me back to my room. They called a doctor to come and see me and he checked my chart, did some observations and physical checks and then decided to give me a lecture.

He looked at me sternly and said, 'If you ever, ever do this again, you will be in Royal Park. I will make sure of that myself.'

I thought to myself, I had been there to visit Katie, and I remember thinking that I never ever want to go to Royal Park. He absolutely used shock and awe to dissuade me from doing that again. It worked, that was enough to convince me. When I got out of the hospital, I swore I would never, ever do that again. They put me on anti-depressants to bring me off the overdose, and all the nerve tablets I had been on for months and months. When you are on that many tablets for that long you cannot just go 'cold turkey'. You have to be on some medication to wean you off them.

You soon realise that when you take all these tablets and you party on constantly, life seems so fantastic and easy and you live in a false reality, but it is your reality. However, when there is no alcohol and no drugs to numb the pain, you suddenly see the real world and all the terrible things in your life. That is when it all becomes all too hard, and you regress back to what makes everything okay again; the drugs and the alcohol. You revert to your false reality, where everything is hazy, with no pain and life is okay.

I never had a mother, my Dad didn't want to talk to me anymore, and my boyfriend wasn't coming back. I didn't have any real friends. I was living in a foreign town and state. Life was shit so what else did I have?

17. Sort Life Out

Once I had come off the drugs, I decided that I needed to get a job, work hard, and save up and get back to Mackay, my hometown. My safe place. I needed to sort my life out. I needed to see Dad, hug him, feel his strong arms around me, feel safe again, and tell him that I love him, and to thank him for everything he has done for me. I haven't seen him for three years. I missed him terribly. To do this I needed to get out of Sale, and extricate myself from all those people, and situations that took me down the ugly path of drug abuse, and self-destruction. Donna, my surrogate Mum, decided to help me and she rang one of her other daughters, who lived in Melbourne, and asked if she could come and collect me, take me back with her to live at her place for a while, and see if she could get me a job down there as a bar attendant.

As soon as I went to Melbourne, I nervously rang my Dad. I am pretty sure Donna had rung him and told him about my alcohol abuse and drug overdose.

When he answered the phone, he said, 'Hi, love I am glad you called, as I have been wanting to talk to you.'

He then proceeded to give me a fatherly lecture, however, he was pleased I had got out of it, and trying to clean myself up and get home. It gave me so much joy and relief to hear his voice, and know he still loved me.

Although I hated the big city, moving to Melbourne worked out really well. Donna's daughter, Carly, who was a caring and lovely person, and was married, worked at the Duke of Kent, where there was an available room, so I moved in there. Her friend, George, worked at the Royal Arcade Hotel, and he gave me a job as a bar attendant, and it was only 3 tram stops away. I met her other sister, Maureen, another caring and lovely woman, also married, and lived in Watsonia. The whole family took me in, and treated me like a sister, and I felt like I belonged somewhere, and had people to rely on if needed.

I often caught the train out to her place for the weekend. I needed a bit of a break away from my three-by-three room, and the rapid pace of the city. There was one night I managed to catch the wrong train. I was running late, and sprinting to the platform for the train I had to catch. There was a train ready to leave, so I leapt in and sat down. Made it or so I thought. As I was slightly late, by a few seconds, I had missed my usual train, and jumped on the next one, not even looking at the signs telling me where the train was going but thinking I had just made it. It turned out the train I was on was going to a different destination, and I ended up in Preston, which is three quarters of an hour drive from Watsonia. It was about eleven pm. I hopped off the train in pitch dark, so scared, and no idea where I was.

I saw a CUB sign, (a pub sign – Carlton United Brewery), in the distance. I was running for my life through these dark streets. I was so scared. I was crying all the way, where am I? I didn't know where I was.

I got into the hotel and asked the bouncer at the door, 'Where am I?'

He said with a puzzled look, 'You're in Preston. love.'

I asked if I could use their phone, and I rang Maureen. She answered the phone, worried and I explained where I was.

She said, 'How the hell did you get there?'

I said, 'I swear, I caught the same train that I catch every weekend.'

She explained to me that there are two platforms, and often there can be two trains leaving the station at the same time but veer off in different directions. She told me stay put, and sent her husband, Dave, to get me. I think I might have ordered a drink to calm myself down. They didn't get mad at me, actually they thought it was quite funny, however, I didn't see the funny side, not until I had calmed down, and felt safe. Lovely people. They really looked after me. Stupid me did the same trick on the Tram.

Kathy Howie

I left work one night, got on the Tram, and it didn't stop at my stop, and I thought it might stop at the next stop. No, it didn't stop again. Oh well, maybe the next stop. To my astonishment, it went past four more stops. Nearly ended up at Royal Park. No thanks.

I went up to the conductor and asked, 'Why haven't you stopped at Little Lonsdale Street?'

He said, 'Did you pull the chain?'

I said, 'No, what chain?'

He let me know I had to pull a chain to let him know to stop at that particular stop. Man, I had caught the same tram for about a month without pulling a chain, and it always stopped. Obviously, other people were pulling the chain for the same stop as mine.

Working behind the bar was very busy, and hard. Being a city hotel, I had customers five deep at the bar non-stop, especially on Fridays and Saturdays. I had to constantly chain pour beer, which is just pouring beer after beer, and sometimes pouring four beers in one hand, from ten am to two pm, with only a half hour break from two to two thirty pm, and then worked until seven pm without any other break.

I worked there for about three months, and my boss' son, Jack, used to come in regularly. Very friendly, and a nice guy I thought. He thought I was pretty nice too. He had these beautiful blue eyes and long eye lashes. I thought he was so gorgeous, and I was smitten. We would have regular chats when he came in, and he got the courage to ask me out, and he invited me up to his mum's place. His mum had remarried. She lived in a little town called Trentham. They owned racehorses and lived in this huge house with eight fireplaces. There was a fireplace in every bedroom, and every other room in the house, except the toilet. It really was a beautiful house, and I had never seen anything like it.

One of their racehorses was called Abstraction. He had won the XXXX Cup, the Albury Cup, and a couple of other major cups in one year. They have a home name for racehorses, and Abstraction's name was Prinny. Later on, when he had retired from racing, a guy from America bought him, and took him to America, and he was in the movie Black Beauty.

18. New Love

Jack and I started dating after that weekend. For my birthday he bought me this great big, gigantic stuffed St Bernard dog. It was so big that in my tiny three by three room, I had to have it either on the bed or on the floor, so I had room to walk around. I don't know what possessed him to get me that. It was gorgeous though, and I loved it. I decided to move in with him, and his father, in a little flat in Surrey Hills. After we had been living together for two years, I fell pregnant, which wasn't part of the plan. Jack's dad was a very heavy smoker and drinker. When I was three months pregnant, we decided to move out, and got a place of our own, as we didn't feel it was a healthy environment to raise a child. We had lived with Jack's dad for about six months. It was so great to have our own place. We lived in Camberwell, a very nice suburb of Melbourne. I was also a heavy smoker, but I gave up while I was pregnant.

We decided to get engaged when I was about eight months pregnant. I think we felt it was the right thing to do, and everything was going well. We had a wonderful party. Donna and all her family came down from Sale. I felt as though I had finally found my place,

Kathy Howie

and belonged to a loving family, I had been craving all my life. I was determined to give my child all my love and be the best mother and wife I could be. There was some trepidation, as the dream of saving up and moving back to Mackay was becoming ever more distant.

I had my beautiful son, Wayde, on the 18th November 1980. Straight away I understood the meaning of unconditional love, which made me wonder if my mother ever felt that. You carry this human inside you for nine months, and then bang, here he is. He was in my arms, and I looked down at him, Gorgeous boy. Spitting image of his father. Beautiful blue eyes, long eye lashes and black hair.

Everything was fine for a year or so, until Jack started drinking quite heavily. A bit too much for my liking. Some nights he would come home at ten pm from his mate's place, and I would have tea ready for him in the oven. After a while I was getting sick of it. For instance, on my birthday, I said I was dying to go out for a dance and a few drinks.

He turned around and said, 'I don't even like dancing.'

I said, 'When we were dating you loved dancing.'

He turned around to me and said, 'I hate dancing. I've got you now, I don't have to dance or take you out.' He got the shits with this, and rang up my friend, Carly, and said, 'For Christ's sake, take Kathy out can you.'

She came over and picked me up and took me to a place called, "Top of the Town", in Doncaster. This was a disco for middle aged people. We had a ball. A couple of weeks later, my girlfriend, Kerry came down from Mackay. She lived with me at Cromer House and we had been mates since we were fifteen. I had such a good time with Carly at the "Top of the Town", I thought I would take Kerry there. Before we left for our big night out, we were getting dressed. I put on these black tights and a long top.

I said to Kerry, 'Does this look good?'

She turned around, laughed so hard she fell on the bed convulsing. I had a second look in the mirror and realised I looked like this cartoon character called, Swamp. Swamp is a bird with long skinny legs. We were laughing so much the neighbour banged on the wall and told us to shut up.

After that Kerry said to me, 'What do you think of my hair, I have just had it permed. Well, what do think? Do you think it makes me look older?'

Being the good friend that I was, I told her it looked beautiful.

We went out and Kerry said to me when we sat down, 'Are you sure my hair doesn't make me look older?'

Of course I said no. I reckon within five minutes, this suave but older looking guy comes up, and asks her for a dance and I swear, after a closer look, he would have been seventy. She gave me this death stare as she went on the dance floor with him, and I started laughing and couldn't stop. I must point out here, that we were only twenty-five at the time.

When Wayde was about two, Jack had this massive car accident, and wrote off our new Statesman that we had bought. He was extremely lucky, as his head went through the windscreen, and for the next six months, I was plucking out tiny pieces of glass. He had lost control, and hit a streetlight pole in Doncaster, which cost us one thousand dollars for the street pole alone, plus the repairs to the vehicle. His drinking had been getting increasingly out of control, and he was getting verbally abusive.

I told Jack I had had enough, and I needed a break, and had to get out of there. I had to go and see Dad. I hadn't seen him for five years, and he hadn't met his grandson, Wayde, yet. I explained to him that if I don't see my dad before he dies, I would leave him. It must have hit home, as the next Friday, Jack brought home a ticket for me and Wayde to go to Mackay a month later. I was so excited and screamed with delight. I was finally getting back to Mackay to see Dad, and he was going to meet his grandson, Wayde, for the first time. I did not know at the time, but Jack had borrowed the money off a friend to pay for the plane tickets.

That very night he bought the ticket home, I was in the bath relaxing, thinking about all the things we would do in Mackay, when Jack came in and said there was a phone call from my sister in Mackay. It seemed urgent, so I got out of the bath, and was standing there, on the phone, wrapped in a towel when my sister told me that Dad had had a massive heart attack.

Living In Fear Of Enemies

My excitement quickly changed to despair and panic, so I got on the phone and changed my flights for the very next morning. I had to pay a bit extra to make the change, but I didn't care I needed to get home.

19. Sadness

We flew up to Mackay the next morning, a Saturday. All the way praying that Dad would be alright. As we exited the plane, I immediately felt the warmth of the sun, and a warm tropical breeze of Mackay that I had long yearned for. I was home. My brother-in-law picked us up from the airport, and we drove past the Mackay Base Hospital.

He asked me, 'Did you want to go and see your Dad now?'

I said, 'No let's go and pick my sister up first.'

My sister decided that we would have lunch first, and then head to the hospital. She had fish and chips ready to eat. I did not feel like anything to eat at that time and getting extremely frustrated that my sister didn't appear to be in any sort of hurry. I just wanted to get to the hospital. Halfway through our fish and chips the hospital rang, and said dad was deteriorating quickly, so we hopped in the car and raced straight to the hospital. We frantically rang the bell in ICU for quite a while. No response. Again, we frantically pressed the button. No response. We saw a nurse heading our way, and she came out with a forlorn look, and promptly advised us dad had passed away.

I was devastated, angry, in disbelief and just crumbled into a mess. I composed myself and went in. When I saw him lying there, breathless, and motionless I just broke down, and started screaming.

'Five @#$&* years. Five @#$&* years since I had seen him.'

My sister was trying to tell me to keep my voice down, but I couldn't help myself. I was so angry at myself, and it seemed as though my world had ended, and once again, I felt lost and helpless. What made it even more difficult was that dad and I had been talking on the phone about once a week for a few months by this stage. Our relationship was back on track, and that was the reason I wanted to go home and see him with Wayde. He was so proud of me and kept saying how he couldn't wait to see the little 'bruiser' (Wayde). He wanted to take him to the beach, fishing, crabbing, to all the wonderful places Mackay had, and do all those things he did with me as a child.

It just filled me with such emptiness, sorrow, and heartache that dad never got to meet his "little bruiser", and I never got to feel his strong arms around me again and hug him. "My beautiful father", I called dad, and his friends affectionately called him 'Blub'. Love you, dad.

We returned to my sister's place, and I ended up staying there for a week, even though I was only supposed to be there for a few days. I didn't care though as I was happy to never go back to be honest. We had to attend to the arduous task of finding dad's will. We went to every bank in Mackay to find this will. We finally found it at Mackay Permanent Building Society. One of the banks I went to was where my good friend Kerry worked. I wasn't in the mood for talking or socialising. I couldn't even talk to her for that long, as it upset me too much. I didn't even see any more of her that trip.

When we read his will it seemed a little surprising, because dad had planned and paid for his funeral and had a bank account for his four children with $600 in each one. It shocked me because dad didn't seem to be the most frugal person with his money, and by this stage of his life, he was on the pension. Do you know what else was weird, dad had always taken a Lotto ticket every Saturday, and he would often say that the day he would win would be the day he dies. The Saturday he passed away, his Lotto numbers won 2nd Division, and he won $600.

To Jack's credit, he flew up to support me, and attend the funeral. We had the funeral in Mackay, at the Catholic Church. It was a beautiful day, and we all got dressed and headed off to the Church. We got to the Church, and someone had commented, and asked where was John, was he coming? Sarah and I looked at each other in astonishment eyes wide, and mouths open.

She said, 'I locked all the doors and the last I heard, he was having a shower.'

We all said, 'Oh my God, he is locked in.'

Those days, doors were locked with a key from the outside. We all started to just burst out in laughter. Other attendees looked at us with dismay, and it must have appeared so strange. He we are supposedly in mourning, and I think we were in such a wound up, sad and nervous state, that John's predicament was little a circuit breaker. We could not refrain from laughing. My brother-in-law went back to get him. My sister and I had to exit the church and sit in the car for a bit to stop laughing. Dad would have thought it was so funny, and we could practically hear him laughing in his coffin. When my brother-in-law picked up John, he just said you "Buddy Bastards", and he said it again when he got to the church.

After the funeral and we had finalised the will, I then flew back to Melbourne with Jack. I didn't want to go, and everyone was so sad, and miserable, and it was the longest flight ever.

20. Heart Broken

Living back in Melbourne, I threw myself into work, and I worked at four different pubs. The Royal Arcade Hotel, The Lord Cecil, The Golden Age, and Ashleigh's Bar. Ashleigh's was well known as a gay hang out; however I was not aware of this. My boss decided to send me to Ashleigh's as they needed a hand. What an experience and a half this shift would turn out to be. Initially things were going well, and it felt like I was working at any other bar. However, the patrons were so friendly, lovely and polite, and it was a pleasure to work there. I was well into my shift, and I noticed in particular, the female patrons were ever so nice to me, and as I passed them their change, they would briefly hold my hand, and I thought, how wonderful these people are here so friendly. It still hadn't dawned on me that they were gay. It was so refreshing, and I was thinking I might have to ask the boss for a transfer and work there full time.

About two o'clock in the morning, I had a break, I sat on the other side of the bar, and saw two women kissing, then the penny dropped, now I get it, now I know where I am. I saw my boss the next day, and he started laughing hysterically, and thought it was just hilarious, because he knew I didn't know what type of bar it was. I realized though that these people were harmless and just gorgeous. They lived in their own little world, and they didn't appear to want to hurt anyone, and just have fun and dance. There were no bar fights, no swearing, and no yelling. They loved life, that's for sure.

It became clear that coming from an isolated North Queensland country town, like Mackay, and going to the big city, was a real eye opener and educational. The city showed you so many different types of people, different lifestyles, different hairdos with wild colours, shaved heads, mohawks and some even spiked. Mackay was a real hick country town when I left, and people like this would not be welcome. That was back in the days when gay people were misunderstood and not accepted, and had to live in secrecy, even in cities. Thank goodness times have changed, and things are different now, where gay people are more widely accepted, however, there is still less of an acceptance in country towns. They now have gay marriages, and can adopt children, and go about their lives like all of us. I was unaccepting, and I guess scared of gay people, but working in Melbourne, and particularly at Ashleigh's, showed me that we need to accept people for who they are.

After dad had passed, I lived in Melbourne for another year. I was extremely unhappy there and longed for Mackay. Arguing constantly with Jack, due to his excessive drinking, and verbal abuse. It got that bad we were sleeping in separate beds for ten months. The love was slowly evaporating. I decided that I needed a holiday in Mackay, and let Jack know I had booked flights. I couldn't afford flights for my son, Wayde, so I made the difficult choice to leave him with Jack while I went up to Mackay for a week. It saddened me greatly, and I waved goodbye to my son, with tears in my eyes. I needed this break to clear my head, and make some hard decisions. I decided to stay with Sarah, my sister.

I went into town to the bank where my friend Kerry worked, to surprise her. She said this was wonderful, and it just so happened that she had a week off. We decided we would go up to the Whitsunday Islands. I needed the holiday, and Kerry needed some stress relief. We spent three nights and four days in the region, and it was just beautiful. One night we spent in a tent at Airlie Beach. A crooked tent at that, I might add. Our tent was up but we seemed to have one metal bar left over. Where did that belong? We noticed a guy camping near us who had the same tent as us, and his looked completely different to ours. Oh well.

Then we spent two nights on Hamilton Island. Beautiful weather, warm breezes, palm trees and we enjoyed cocktails, wine, champagne, and just lived it up, and forgetting about our lives for a short period of time. Even had a cigar. It was definitely the life, and just what we both needed. I think, if I was trapped in a cardboard box with my friend Kerry, we would still be having a ball. We just always had so much fun together. We laughed a lot, all the time, and we fed off each other's silly mistakes, stories or sayings. However, our fun was soon short lived, and I had to pack up, and head back to Melbourne. It was sad, that after such a wonderful week in Mackay, to have to leave and go back to Melbourne.

My thoughts were filled with memories of all my

good times, and the amazing week in Mackay. However, they soon became consumed by thoughts of returning to Melbourne, and the bad times, and mixed emotions of what was there for me. The bright light was seeing my beautiful boy again. I got back to Melbourne, after my trip to Mackay, and my Whitsunday escape with Kerry, got off the train, and this guy had nicely asked me if I needed a hand to get my port down from the port rack. I replied yes please, how lovely was that I thought. What a gentleman. As I hopped off the train the guy said, there you go love. Jack was there waiting for me, and saw the gentleman assisting me.

Jack was into me straight away and got heated and said, 'Who was that?'

I tried to explain that I didn't know him, he is just a nice guy who helped me with my port.

He said, 'Yeah I bet.'

He was so angry with me he wouldn't talk to me all the way home. He didn't even ask, nor was even interested, in how my trip was, and what I did. I started to think this was not what I needed in my life. Oh, take me back to Mackay, away from this miserable place.

Not long after I got back to Melbourne, friends of Kerry's, Lyle and Steve, who I had been introduced to in Mackay, had ridden their motorbikes down to Melbourne to visit other friends of theirs. They decided to call in and see me. They looked so handsome and dangerous in their black leathers. I was so excited to see some friends from Mackay and gave them big hugs.

Jack immediately saw red and became suspicious and accused me of playing around on him whilst in Mackay. I tried to convince him that I hadn't done anything wrong and was totally innocent. His jealousy was never ending and escalating.

I missed Mackay terribly, the beaches, the warmth, the sun and the friends, and the relaxed slow pace of a country town. The time had come; enough was enough. Time to do some serious thinking that I really needed to make a big change in my life and my son's. I found the courage to tell Jack that I didn't love him anymore, and I could no longer live in Melbourne, and I was packing up and going back home to Mackay. Jack, understandably, was not very happy with my decision. I was not only leaving him, but I was taking away his son. For that I felt extremely guilty, however, I had to put me first and do what was best for me for a change. I told him that I would not seek any child maintenance, as I was taking his son away, and I felt so guilty.

It got so bad that one night we had a massive argument, and I got so scared that he might get violent. I tried to talk him down but soon realised I had to get away from him. I bolted out of the house and I was running down the street looking back to see if he was coming. He had stopped running returned to the house and jumped in the car and he was looking for me in the car. Somehow, he found me as I was hiding in a car park, down this lane way. He pulled up motioned for me to get in the car. I got in the car and went back home with him, and he calmed down. We sat down, and I told him I have to leave; I couldn't stay there any longer. I even said to him, don't you realise we have not been sleeping together for the last ten months. He gave me this confused look as if he was oblivious to what was going on in our lives.

It was as if he had his little woman at home to feed him and keep the house tidy, and that this was somehow normal. He reluctantly agreed, and we sold all the furniture, and he was kind enough to give me all of the money from the sale so that Wayde and I could fly to Mackay.

I had little money, a couple of suitcases of belongings, but finally I was going home to Mackay, and I had my boy.

21. Single Motherhood

When I got on that one-way flight to Mackay, I settled Wayde in, buckled myself in, and just put my head back on the head rest. I let out a huge sigh with a feeling of euphoria and just pure relief. I am going home to my safe place, Mackay. We arrived, Hooray!

When we landed, I had the big dog that Jack had given me under one arm, and Wayde was in the other arm. I bounced down those stairs and into the terminal with a purpose in life I had not felt for a long time, smiling broadly.

When we went and picked up my port, this guy walking past said, 'What's in the port, pal?'

I just laughed so hard. That was a nice light-hearted welcome back to Mackay, and a bit of country humour.

I stayed at my sister's place for a short time until I found somewhere to live. My good friend Kerry rang me up one day and said there was a nice duplex in Vicky Court, on the north side of Mackay. I decided to check it out and ended up moving in there. My bikie, leather-bound friends, Lyle and Steve, looked for a car for me, and found a little Ford Cortina. It was green, with one bright orange guard. The seats looked all tattered and torn. There was a rust spot under the driver's seat. I could see the ground as I drove. Much like the Flintstones car. For two hundred and fifty dollars what do you expect. It got me around though and served its purpose. It never ever broke down, but I was always on the side of the road with a flat tyre. Got good at changing tyres. Steve and his brother, Stuey, were so kind that they bought me a TV unit. So wonderful to have people that cared for me in my life.

Steve often took Wayde for little bike rides on his huge motorbike. Wayde looked scared at first, with his little helmet on. He clung on tightly to Steve with both arms wrapped around his torso. When he came back you could not wipe the smile from his little face, and his excitement was treasurable.

I decided to get Wayde involved in sport and got him into BMX bike racing. Every Saturday morning, we would go to the BMX track at Cremorne. Wayde loved sports and had no fear. During one race he was madly pedalling and up the front of the field, when he crashed, and face-planted into the track. He had scratches, grazes, and gravel rash, but the little trooper kept going, Of course I was panicking thinking he had broken everything.

Sunday mornings I often took Wayde to the beach at the Harbour, and he loved the outdoors. There was one day we were playing chasey, he was running behind me trying to get me, and I was swerving left to right, left to right, he tripped on my heel. I had my bikinis on, and he grabbed my bikini bottoms on the way down, and I ended up butt naked in the middle of Harbour beach. There was a guy running past at the same time, and he started laughing. You soon learn there is only so much two hands can cover whilst pulling your pants up at the same time, and Wayde still had hold of them and wouldn't let go. So embarrassing, but we laughed later on.

Three months after I had moved to Mackay, Jack decided to come to Mackay for a visit to see us. I was pleased he was making the effort to come, and Wayde was so excited. He had lost all his weight, was fit, and he looked really good then. He travelled up to try and reconcile with me, but once love is gone, it is gone, you can't regain it again, and there was no way I was returning to Melbourne. After he went back to Melbourne, he kept ringing me, but it was when he was drunk, and at about three o'clock in the morning. I would wake up answer the phone knowing exactly who it was, and I would beg him to please ring his son at an appropriate time, don't ring me I am not interested.

He would tell me how much he missed me, and loved me, and wanted me back. It broke my heart, because some nights Wayde would be sitting on the side of his bed looking at a photo of his father. and crying and asking, when his dad was coming to see him. Every now and again, I would send Wayde down to see his dad for a holiday, as I knew Wayde needed his father in his life.

There was two Christmases I had sent Wayde down to Melbourne to see his father.

The second time Wayde came back, I was sitting at the table and he said, 'It's all your fault.'

I said, 'What is my fault, darling'?

He said, 'That I don't live with my daddy.' He told me that, 'Daddy would live with you, but you don't want to live with him. Daddy said to me, "It is your mother's fault".'

I decided that's it, he doesn't need to see his son anymore. I am not going to waste my money sending him down there when I have never asked for child maintenance. I found out later that Jack would often leave Wayde with Carly, or other friends when in Melbourne, and he would hardly see him. I thought, I can raise Wayde as a single parent.

Jack seemed more interested in me than in his own son and was still ringing at ungodly hours of the morning drunk. For example, later in Wayde's life, when he was about six, one Christmas, Jack had decided to travel around Australia.

He finally rang Wayde and said, 'When I get to Darwin, I will fly you up and we will go on this big fishing trip and catch heaps of Marlin.'

Wayde was so excited, as he loved fishing, and he told all the kids at school that he was going on this big fishing trip. Christmas had come, Christmas had gone, and we heard nothing from Jack. Wayde remained hopeful and I was trying to support him knowing his father would let him down. My poor son, the first day back at school he started crying.

I said to him, 'What's wrong, Darling'.

He said, 'I told all the kids at school I was going on this big trip. What am I going to say to them now?'

I felt so disappointed for him and I could hear the anguish in his voice, so I said, 'Just lie, Darling, tell them you went on this fishing trip and caught heaps of Marlin'.

Not the best advice I know. I shouldn't get my son to lie, but what do you do? I was so sick of my son being let down, and upset because of his father, but he loved him, and wanted him in his life.

The next time I saw Jack, it was about two months later, I was walking out of the Social Security in Mackay, and to my absolute surprise he was walking in. I had to do the double take. We passed each other on the steps. I asked him where the hell had he been, and when did he arrive in Mackay. He wouldn't offer any explanation where he had been, what he had been doing or why he was here. He decided to stay here and ended up living in Mackay for quite a few years. He met a lovely lady, Lisa. They ended up getting married and Jack made Wayde his Best Man. Wayde was about thirteen by then.

Anyway, back to the earlier years. I had applied for a housing commission unit, which was much more affordable rent, and I finally got one near Queens Park. My neighbour had a girl the same age as Wayde, and they got on really well. I started work at the Metropolitan Hotel. I was getting part pension, and part work at the time. Initially my neighbour would mind Wayde, however, I was a little bit concerned as she had a drug habit, and felt she was a bad influence as Wayde bought home a bong which was made out of an orange juice bottle and a hose that he had found at the BMX track. I was furious and decided to look for other childminding services.

I eventually found this babysitter in the newspaper. One dollar per hour. Ok, me being me, still young and wanting a social life and going out on Friday and Saturday night, I decided to meet this babysitter, and went around to see her. Her name was Kay. She was so lovely, married and had three girls. Wayde was the same age as the middle girl. Kay is a beautiful, kind lady.

I asked her, 'Why is it so cheap?'

She said, 'Because I have three children, and I can't afford to go out, and even if I wanted to go out it would cost me thirty dollars an hour for a babysitter.'

We then agreed that if I fed Wayde, and had him ready for bed, I would take him to Kay's place, and he would sleep there the night, and she would only charge me twenty dollars. Wayde loved it there and was there so often he called her Aunty Kay and Uncle Matt, and because they had three girls, they used to think of him as their little boy, and treated him like their own son and the girls like he was a brother. Matt would play the guitar with him. He would play in the mud, and drains with his adopted sisters, Kay's girls, as I did as a kid with my friends. Kay and I became great friends, and at times she even called me her little sister, and her kids would call me Aunty. From then to now, they still call me Aunty. We are still great friends to this day.

22. Third Time Lucky in Love

I commenced working as a bar attendant at the Metropolitan Hotel. There I met this guy. His name was Macca. Macca had long curly dark hair, brown eyes, and a gentle nature. Lovely guy, and Wayde loved him too. He treated me so well, and we dated for four years. Macca played Australian Rules Football for the Swans (Mackay) Football Club. As soon as Wayde turned six, I got him playing football with him. Wayde loved him so much, the same question arose again, just as it did when I was at Jonesy's. Wayde asked if he could call Macca, Daddy. Macca said no, you only have one daddy. The same answer I got from Jonesy when I asked if I could call her mum. As I write this now, it suddenly dawned on me the disappointment Wayde must have felt. I know how I felt.

When I was thirty years old, I was getting really bad pains in my stomach. I decided to go to the Doctor's and get checked out and he gave me a smear test. Of course, I had to wait a few days for the results. I got a phone call from the Doctor saying he wanted to see me straight away. Urgently. When I went in, he said I had CIN2 in the cervix.

I asked, 'What is that?'

He said, 'It is called Cancer In Neutral'.

I just slumped in the chair and thought, *Oh no, the big C, Jack the Dancer*. I then had to go and see a Specialist, and he advised that I needed to get the cancer cells burnt off. Of course, it meant a day in hospital for the treatment. I asked him what happens if I don't get this operation done. He said, well, we are talking about cancer here. What do you think will happen? In my mind, I was saying, give me a god damn break. I was back in Mackay, my son was happy in school, and playing sport, and I had a nice boyfriend. I decided to have the operation, and then I had to have monthly follow up checks.

Six months later it was back. I had to get those cells burnt out again. Monthly checks again, and low and behold, three months after that operation, it was back again. Viciously this time. Stage 4 by this time. Another operation, and this time they decided to do a Cone Biopsy. There was a big cancer spot on my cervix, as well as burning the rest of the cells that were around it. Wow, life's a bitch.

As I was on the pill at the time, the doctor said to work out whether I wanted to have any more children or not. Big decision, however, as I was thirty years old, perhaps my time was over to have more children. He thought it was best to tie my tubes so I could get off the pill. He really thought that it was causing the cancer. The doctor did advise that cancer can be hereditary, so he asked me to check if Cervical Cancer ran in my family. I asked my sister, and she told me yes, my dad's sister had died at seventeen from Cervical Cancer. It was my Aunty Flo's twin, who would have been forty years older than me. In those days, they probably never had a cure. I couldn't bear the thought of Wayde not having his mother, so I decided to have the operation to get my tubes tied, and I didn't have to take the pill anymore. It hasn't returned since, thank goodness.

Before I entered hospital, I had found this black crow on the side of the road. He was injured. I thought he might have been hit by a car. While I was in hospital, I told my boyfriend, Macca, not to forget to feed the black crow, that I was trying to get back on its feet. I had him in a cage, and I was feeding him mince. He seemed to come good, and I thought he might be ready to be released after I got out of hospital. Macca forgot to feed him, and of course I came home to find a dead bird. I had him for about three months. *Why can't life go smoothly for me?*

Then about two years later I had this terrible tooth ache. I went to the dentist and found out I had an abscess on my tooth. He put me on antibiotics for a week, and I returned to the dentist still in pain. He then decided to take x-ray's, which showed that I still had a baby tooth, and under that was the second tooth that had grown sideways. What a mess. This was in my bottom jaw. Here I go again. Off to hospital to get that removed. This is my seventh operation so far in my life. It was not fun at all. I couldn't smile for a while until the stitches dissolved. It was annoying me so much, I decided to cut them out myself with a razor blade. After four weeks I was successful getting them out.

Life went on as normal for a little while. My relationship with my sister had improved, and we were in a pretty good place. When I wasn't working, I would take Wayde to kindergarten, and finish my housework, and then go to my sister's place, and help her with her housework. I was always doing her dishes from the night before and vacuuming. I didn't mind because I had grown to love her and was happy to help. She was the only family I had left.

I went down to the shops one day, and a friend of hers said to me, 'Are you proud of yourself? Sleeping with your brother-in-law?'

That word "slut" surfaced again. Well, you could imagine my reaction, and I was in total shock. I went over to my sister's place and faced her with it.

Her answer to that was, 'You always said you loved him, so that's what I told people'.

I said, 'Yeah, when I was a kid. And as a brother-in-law, not a boyfriend. He's your husband for God's sake.'

Quite a few years later, while my sister was still alive, I happened to be in an elevator visiting a friend at hospital. A good friend of my sister's just happened to be in the same elevator.

They turned to me and said, 'It is a shame your sister can't forgive you.'

I turned to her with a scornful look and said, 'For

what? There is nothing to forgive. My sister is sick in the head. I never, ever, slept with my brother-in-law.'

Again, so many years later, I felt so humiliated, angry, and disgusted with her. Dad had always said, in my younger days, that my sister was always jealous of me. I didn't believe him, but now I know that she was a jealous psycho.

I was disgusted and I walked out of there in absolute rage, and I never saw, or spoke to, her after that day, for twenty years. I felt so embarrassed, humiliated, and upset, as people believed her lies, and so I would get filthy looks from her friends. I thought, if this is what a sister can do to her sibling, then I don't want a sister. She died without me ever speaking to her again and we never reconciled. I didn't care though. Good riddance. How disgusting, to spread vicious lies and accusations about me to not only one person, but all her friends, which were some of my friends too.

I think I must have developed a four-year itch, or something as I started falling out of love with Macca. He was doing the same thing as Jack, staying out with his mates, and drinking and not coming home. I have got to stop meeting and dating customers at work. Macca was a bit damaged, as he was involved in a serious car accident that killed his previous girlfriend, and he kind of blamed himself. He struggled with that, and he never drove a car again, and only rode a pushbike from that day on. His drinking escalated. We ended up splitting up after about four years and both of us were okay with the split, and he understood. Wayde did not take this very well though, as Macca had grown on him, and became a father figure in his life. Has was quite upset for a while. Kept asking me where was Macca? Why isn't he coming around? Wayde was six years old at this stage. It was really hard for me to make excuses as to why he wasn't coming around. I never put Macca down in front of Wayde though. But we think children are resilient in cases like this, however, I know it hurt him terribly.

Then I met Scott. He was twenty-one years old and I was thirty-one. It only lasted three months because he was an absolute psycho and control freak. We would go out, and he was so insanely jealous. One night we were standing at a table in a club, and he had his back to the dance floor. I was facing it. I was looking at an old friend dancing behind him, and I was waving and smiling at her, yelling out, how you going?

Scott turned to me and said, 'Who the hell are you looking and smiling at now?'

I thought, *oh my God, this can't be happening again.*

I said to him, 'Turn around and have a look.'

He said, 'I wouldn't embarrass myself.'

It was a girl I went to school with. That night, I thought, *that's it, I am over this shit.* On the way home he started getting really vicious, with an almost evil look on his face, as if he was going to hit me. I was telling him we were breaking up. He kept saying, no we were not. I got my back up, and I thought, no, the break-up is coming on now. I said to Scott I am going to take him home, and we were finished. I took him home to his unit.

He said, 'No, no, we are going to talk about this.'

I said, 'I don't want to talk about it.'

I let him out of the car, but he made me come inside. He was busting for the toilet which was upstairs.

He roughly pushed me on the chair and said, 'Just sit there. I will be back in a minute. Don't move.'

He was walking up the stairs ever so slowly, I could see his feet through the gaps in the stair treads, and he stopped halfway probably to see what I would do. I was inching closer to the edge of the chair, ready to bolt, as I thought as soon as he gets upstairs, I am going to make a run to my car, get in and lock the doors. Once his feet started moving again and they were out of sight, I leapt off the chair and ran for my life. I managed to make it into the car, and quickly locked all the doors. He must not have gone to the toilet, he ran straight back down those stairs, and jumped on the bonnet of my car, and started bashing the windscreen, yelling, and screaming vile stuff at me.

I slammed the car in reverse, and as I was driving backwards out of his driveway, he was hanging onto the windscreen wipers screaming with devil eyes. I took off down Shakespeare Street in front of his house. I was petrified, my heart was pounding, *what am I going to do?* Surely, he will come off. I was doing about sixty kms per hour, and he was still on the bonnet, defiantly hanging onto the wipers. I thought the only way to get him off was to slam on the brakes. I slammed on those brakes and he slid off the bonnet. The thought briefly crossed my mind to run him over, but the nice person overpowered that thought, and I went around him. I got home, quickly got out of the car, locked it, then raced inside, and locked all the doors. I realised he was going to be around here within minutes, and thought I was not safe there. I bravely decided to make a run for the car and drive over to North Mackay to Kerry's house. I know he didn't know where Kerry lived. I was frantically banging on her door at around four am in the morning. She answered, and I told her about Scott, and what had happened. She said I could sleep there for the night. Within the next hour there was a crazy bashing at the door.

Horrified, I said to Kerry, 'It has to be him.'

She said, 'I am going to fix him up.'

I said 'No, Kerry. You stay here, I will just have to go home with him.'

I thought I was going to have to drive him home, but he had stolen this push bike to get over there. I drove, and he madly rode the push bike, as fast as he could. He was trying hard to keep up to the car as, he was thinking I was trying to go somewhere else. We got to my place and I slumped in my car seat, and I realised I had to sit down and talk to him.

When he got there, we went inside.

First off, I asked him, 'How did you know I was over at my friend's place, and where she lived?'

He said, 'I was trying to break into your flat, and the neighbour rang the police. When the police came around, the neighbour came out and said, Oh it's just you, Scott'.

So, the police helped Scott get the window open, and let him in. Can you believe that! He then got my phone book, and just guessed I was over at Kerry's place, and he got her address from the book. We talked for hours, going around and around in circles. I said I had to go to work at ten am. We talked until nine am. So, I changed and got ready for work, and it wasn't until I left to go to work that he left on his stolen push bike.

He said, 'If I can't go out with you, then I won't be able to stand to see you with anyone else, I am going to have to go back to Perth.'

I think he was trying to make me feel guilty or sorry for him, but good riddance, and I made sure that relationship was well and truly over. I had a sunroof in my car, which I often left open, and at least once a week, I was getting a love letter from him through the roof. Two weeks after that he left and went back to Perth. Ironically, I was taking Wayde to the babysitters on my way to work, I stopped at a set of lights, and a taxi was pulled up beside me, and Scott was in the taxi on his way to the airport. He was waving and smiling trying to get my attention, but I ignored him. I didn't want to even look at him.

23. A Chance Meeting

I was still involved with the footy club, as Wayde was still playing juniors there, which was a bit awkward for a little bit, but most people understood when they found out what went on. One night when I was out at my favourite night club, Paradise Nights, I ran into an opposition player from the North Mackay Saints, the Swan's archrivals. His name was Faz. We ended up like girlfriends, us two. He was such a good friend, for a male. He would come around to my place and get dressed to go out and we would always check that we both looked okay. Faz had moved up from Melbourne, so he was a pretty snappy dresser, and always had product in his hair to have that wet look. Absolutely gorgeous guy. We used to go out and have a ball. One night we were out at, *Paradise Nights*, and his mate, a tall guy that had blonde ringlets, blue eyes, came up to us while we were talking. I had this bright green, fluorescent shirt on.

Faz's mate said to me, 'Have you got sunglasses to hand out while you are wearing a top like that?'

Unusual pick-up line but I thought, *wow, he is*

nice. As he walked away, I was giving him the up and down look with my eyes.

I turned around to Faz and said, 'Who was that?'

Faz just brushed it off and said, 'Ah, don't worry about him, that's just Dog.'

I said, 'What? Dog?'

He said, 'Yeah, that's his nickname, that's what everyone calls him.'

I thought to myself, how on earth can a gorgeous guy like that be called Dog. I think we chatted that night and continued to run into each other most weekends, and other nights. I started to get to know this guy, and started talking to him more, and found out his real name was Rohan. We started dating. I discovered his age was twenty-four at the time, and I didn't realise he was so young. I was thirty-one at the time.

I introduced him to my son, Wayde, who was seven at the time. Wayde was a bit shy at first. Rohan played Aussie Rules Football for the North Mackay Saints, and Wayde played for the Eastern Swans. Rohan started taking Wayde to his junior football games, which was the opposition team for Rohan. He was a bit uncomfortable going there, but he felt Wayde needed a father figure in his life, so he always took him.

He said to Wayde one day, 'Maybe you should come and play for the mighty Saints.'

Living In Fear Of Enemies

Rohan never forced him to change teams, but Wayde decided to go to the Saints in the end. Rohan was really good with Wayde, and we ended up putting him in a soccer team as well, as he needed to be kept busy. All up he was in BMX, football, and soccer. Friday and Saturday nights were usually my nights out.

Rohan and I decided to go to a B & S Ball, (Bachelor & Spinsters Ball), in Rockhampton, which our good friend Faz was going to. We piled into my little green Cortina and made the four-hour drive down. We met some other friends from Mackay down there. It was a four-day trip, and the first one hundred people to book, received a free day at the races, which was on the Friday, with free Champagne, beer, wine, and dinner at Duthie's Hotel. We went to Great Keppel Island on Saturday. We had the ball on the Saturday night, and the Recovery Day was on the Sunday. Well, we were so excited, what an amazing weekend ahead. Of course, I should know by now, not to get too excited over anything, because it might not go as I expect. First day at the races was amazing, we met some wonderful people, and a very funny group of guys all dressed and named the same. Dave, Dave, Dave. Dave's everywhere. One of the Dave's and I were dancing on the grass, drinking Champagne, just having a ball.

We were extremely inebriated when we left, and that night, we were out for dinner at Duthie's Hotel. Rohan and I were going to the toilet at the same time, why, I don't know. We decided to take what we thought was a shortcut through a door. We opened the door and instantly we fell down ten cement stairs. Of course, my boyfriend fell on top of me, and practically rode me down the stairs. As I was upside down, motionless, at the bottom of the stairs with my drunken boyfriend on top of me, our mate Faz sat at the top step.

He yelled at me, 'Kathy, come on, you are just trying to get out of your shout.'

I muttered, 'I can't move.'

I couldn't lift myself up as my arm wouldn't move even when my boyfriend managed to get off me.

Faz, sitting at the top of the stairs shaking his head, kept saying, 'Come on, Kathy, you are just trying to get out of your shout'.

By this time, I am screaming. 'I can't move!'

He said, 'No, No, No, No, No excuses, it's your shout.'

Luckily, there was a nurse who saw what had happened, and she came down the stairs to comfort and assess. You can guess, I broke my funny bone, I had a massive hematoma to the head, which resulted in concussion, and a lump on my leg, badly bruised. I managed to make my way to the hospital with the help of Rohan, who was so drunk he wasn't much use. The doctors felt it was best if I stayed in hospital. I told them that's no good, as I was on a four-day B&S trip. I told them I would just take it easy for the rest of the weekend. After finally convincing them I would be alright, they decided to keep me there for the rest of the night, and they said I could get out in the morning. They could only give me Panadol as my alcohol reading was too high for any other pain killers.

The next day was our trip to Great Keppel Island. I said I might stay in the caravan, and Rohan said if I wasn't going that he would stay with me. I didn't want to spoil their trip, so I decided to go along, and who knows, a boat trip to an island might be relaxing. It was a beautiful day and Rohan, Faz and I had a good time. On the boat over to the island, Faz was eating a packet of chips, he was standing up with Rohan, and I was sitting on the seat feeling pretty crook. Faz put his half empty packet of chips on the seat next to me, and I started feeling violently ill. I was too embarrassed to be sick in front of a boat load of people so I picked up his packet of chips and spewed into that.

At the top of his voice, Faz said, 'I didn't want those chips, anyway, did I?'

That of course made everyone else on the boat aware of what I was doing. I was determined to ensure Rohan and Faz had a good day and did everything to make sure of that. I tried to look interested, and not complain, however I was so, so, so sick. I had bad pain in my leg, and I had a severe headache. I really didn't want to go to the Ball that night and would have been happy to stay in bed. I really suffered that weekend. I wanted Rohan to have a good time, and not suffer because of me. Begrudgingly, I managed to have a shower, struggled to put on my glamourous gown, did my hair nicely with one hand, and put on my makeup. Hard to do make-up left-handed when you are right-handed. I reluctantly went to the Ball that night.

When we got to the Ball, I noticed there were a few other injured attendees. There appeared to be a lot of people plastered up or on crutches. I didn't feel lonely anymore or left out. Rohan found me a chair and decided to get me a couple of shots of Sambuca to numb the pain. Then he got me a couple more shots, and the pain subsided, and I started to feel a bit more relaxed. Rohan and Faz decided to go for a walk around the venue, so they made me comfortable, got me a couple more shots and off they went. When Rohan returned, he couldn't find me in my seat and was looking for me everywhere, when Faz spotted me on the dance floor. I was up dancing with a guy with a broken leg, and he was on crutches, and I danced with another guy with a broken collar bone.

Rohan and Faz just laughed. Half the time I sat there, with half my arm in plaster, looking sad and lonely. But all these guys seemed to have sympathy towards me, kneeling in front of me asking what had happened to me. They were saying, "What happened to you? Are you the girl who fell down the stairs at Duthie's last night?" Everyone seemed to know about it. I ended up having a wonderful night and was glad I went along.

The next day, Recovery Day, I thought would be a bit more laid back, people hungover just relaxing in the sun. Well Recovery Day was just as wild as the first day. There was a massive inflatable pool that everyone was jumping in. There were barrels of punch that people were dipping their shoes in to drink out of. It was definitely a B&S Ball we would not forget. The four-hour drive back to Mackay on the Monday seemed to take all day. After my fall, and subsequent injuries, I tried to remain positive, and enjoy myself, and a lot of the time I was laughing so much I had forgotten about the pain.

About two years later, I received a small insurance payout from Duthie's Hotel. I didn't want to waste it, I thought this is my opportunity to finally get ahead in life, and I wanted to put a deposit on a house. I was a bit scared to go it alone, so I asked Rohan if he would help me, not really knowing if our relationship was going to last.

Our relationship was very strong, and I didn't have any problems with it at that time. I was always a bit sceptical, and very cautious about getting too involved. We had a good agreement, that if we split up in the future, we would sell the house, I would get my deposit back, and the rest would be 50/50. We bought this beautiful three-bedroom, high set house, in Andergrove, with a beautiful outdoor BBQ area. Out of Housing Commission and into my own home. Oh my god. My life has changed so much. A boyfriend that really loves me, a gorgeous son, and my own house. It was the first place that I lived in that I could actually call home. I couldn't believe it. What a feeling of freedom.

Rohan and I had a relationship that was so easy, and I felt as though I had finally found my knight in shining armour. Of course, we had our ups and downs, like every couple does. For instance, one night at a footy club function, we had a huge argument, so I left without telling anyone, and decided to walk home by myself in the pitch black of night. Our house was about a half hour walk. Well, the footpath cement was lifted in this one spot, and of course I was walking angrily, and managed to kick the raised cement. I come down like a ton of bricks, and the pain was instantaneous and excruciating. I ended up hobbling to a friend's place close by and stayed there the night. I got home the next day, and Rohan was very hungover, but also extremely worried, as he had no idea where I was. He had called a couple of friends to see if I was there, but I didn't care, as I was still angry with him. I was still in a lot of pain, and so I went to the doctors and yep, you guessed it again, I broke my toe. All he could do was tape that toe to the next one as they can't put your toes in plaster. My fault, stupid me.

Of course, we made up that day once we realised it was something trivial. Anyway, that will teach me to walk home in the dark by myself. On another occasion, around about a year later, Rohan and I went out with our football friends, as was the usual weekend activities. I was dancing on the dance floor, and this girl that I worked with at the time, and who didn't like me, was angry with me for some reason. She pushed me, and I lost my balance and fell hitting my face hard on the floor. I was again in agony and felt like I had been hit by a bus.

She took off very quickly, and left the premises, as some of my friends were keen to exact some revenge. Off we go to the hospital, and they confirmed that my right cheek bone was broken. This is my third broken bone so far. There was no surgery at the time, however, later in life I was advised by another doctor that it should have been operated on and pushed back out. Perhaps the lesson for me should have been don't drink too much and stay at home, but I wouldn't change too much of my party days.

Everything was going fine there for a while. My life seemed to be sorting itself out, and it was incident free, and Rohan and I were forming a strong bond. Rohan and I used to still go out on a Friday and Saturday night, as we enjoyed our nights out with friends. The weekends would be all sports for Wayde, with Footy, cricket, and he rode a motorbike around with mates. Rohan was working Monday – Friday during the day. He would come home, and I would have dinner ready for him and Wayde. We had about thirty minutes and would quickly eat, catch up on the day's news, and then I would go to work, and he would take over the home duties. We had been dating and living together for about four years, and we were just so comfortable in our relationship.

24. Murder Next Door

When I was still living in my housing commission unit, where I had some lovely neighbours. In particular, Joan and Lily, who were a mother and daughter living together. They were a harmless couple who wouldn't hurt anyone. Lily, the mother, was in her eighties, and Joan, the daughter, was in her sixties. Lily would always bring over fresh homemade cupcakes or biscuits. Joan, at five o'clock every morning, would go next door for a walk around Queens Park to collect aluminium cans to supplement their pension. I often warned Joan that walking around Queens Park in the dark was far too dangerous for her, and she would always say in a tough manner, that, "No-one is going to get me. I will give them what for". Joan did this every morning for roughly two years, and there was never any scary moments or issues.

I came home from shopping early one morning only to be greeted by numerous police cars, ambulance, and police officers everywhere. Immediately I went into a state of panic. I noticed the police were congregated in Lily and Joan's unit, so I rushed in there feeling numb and scared. What had happened?

Lily was just inconsolable and screaming out, 'Joan is dead, Joan is dead.'

I screamed, 'What's happened?'

Lily answered, 'She has been murdered in the park'.

I was just stunned and held Lily tight asking questions like, "How, why, when?" Numbness and fear consumed me, as the realisation hit me that there has been a murder next door. Would I be next was my thoughts? Lily was so traumatised that she was taken to the hospital for observation, and to be sedated, and calmed as they were worried about her health, and age, and the shock of the incident.

Joan had been on her usual morning walk through the park, looking for cans, when she was attacked by an unknown assailant, and was later found by a passer-by. She had been severely beaten and subsequently died from her injuries.

The police investigated the crime over the next few days and discovered that the offender was living in units directly opposite the park and had been watching Joan for months. The motive was unknown, as Joan had no money or valuables, and was only carrying a plastic bag full of empty cans.

Lily returned home a few days later to arrange her funeral, which I attended. As thanks for my support, Lily crocheted a lovely blanket for me as, Rohan, Wayde and I were going a road trip to Victoria. The day we returned, from our road trip, we spotted the ambulance out the front of our unit complex. I thought, *what now?* I was told by the ambulance operators, that Lily had passed away alone. So sad.

25. The Proposal

We had discussed marriage, and neither of us were too concerned if we got married or not, so we just let things continue on. Well, one night we got out to our favourite nightclub in Mackay, Paradise Nights, the place we met. Rohan must have all of a sudden had this epiphany, or maybe he was just too drunk, or maybe he had planned it. To this day I am still unsure as he doesn't know either. I reckon it was about three am in the morning, and we were just doing our usual thing dancing, partying with friends, when suddenly, he decided to get down on one knee and propose to me.

I went to hit him on the shoulder, and I pushed him over and said, 'Don't be stupid, get up you idiot.'

It took me by surprise as it was so out of the blue, and I didn't take him seriously. Everyone at our table just stopped and looked at us with mouths and eyes wide open.

He got up and said, 'No, I am serious, I want to marry you.'

I looked at him and said, 'Stop it, you're just drunk.'

He looked a bit perplexed and thought, well, she doesn't think I am serious and didn't believe me, so he decided to go up to the DJ and told the DJ that he asked his girlfriend to marry him, but she doesn't believe him.

So, the DJ announced to everyone, 'Is there a Kathy Wessel here tonight?'

Of course, all of my friends were pointing to me.

He said, 'Your boyfriend has something to say to you.'

The DJ gave him the microphone.

Rohan then said, 'Hey, babe, I am serious. Will you marry me?'

All my friends, with eyes and mouths wide again, composed themselves and started screaming at me, "What are you going to say".

I was yelling out, 'No, he doesn't, he is just drunk,' with an embarrassing smile on my face.

I really thought he was just mucking around, as he has always been a bit of a joker at times. Of, course I said no and gave him another love tap on the shoulder when he returned to the table. We went home that night, and in the taxi, he was still at me to get married.

I said, 'If you are still serious, then ask me in the morning when you are sober.'

So, the next morning, a Sunday, I said to him, 'Do you remember what you asked me last night.'

To my astonishment he remembered and asked me to marry him again.

I said jokingly, 'You are still drunk, ask me tomorrow.'

Then every day, for the next four days he asked me again, and again, and I think he felt by now he was past the point of no return. I even asked his friend, Jacko, if Rohan was serious?

He said 'Yes, I think he is.'

So, I made him wait, and he kept asking. I was working in a bottle shop at the time, so the next Friday, I decided to buy him an eight-year-old Jack Daniels crystal decanter. I went to the florist and bought three balloons, and the balloons spelt, Y E S. I sent it to his work.

In the afternoon, Rohan turned up in his truck at his work, and he was the last driver back to the depot that day. All his fellow workmates knew about the proposal and were also anxiously awaiting my answer. As all the others had returned to the depot before Rohan, they had seen what was on the desk for him, they were gleefully laughing and running out to his truck to help him unload it.

Kathy Howie

Rohan thought it was a bit strange, as they never came to help him like that before, but he welcomed the assistance, especially on a Friday. They always had a couple of beers on a Friday, and he thought the boys were keen today for a beer. A couple of them excitedly said "Come inside quick, there is something for you".

As he walked into the office area of the depot, he immediately saw the decanter and the balloons sitting on his desk. The workmates cheered and shouted, "She said Yes. Kathy said Yes".

He was so happy and excited and rang me up straight away. A few of the boys reckon he had a tear in his eye, but he denied it. They all thought the beers tasted better that day.

The next weekend we went out to go ring shopping, and we both bought rings. Rohan wanted me to pick it out. I was so excited. My life was finally turning around for the better, and I had a future to look forward to with my white knight.

A few weeks later, once the excitement of getting engaged to be married had subsided, I sat down and really thought about what our future would look like. We had our home, and a son to raise.

Then the realisation set in that I couldn't have any more children, because my tubes had been tied.

26. More Grief

Guilt started to enter my thoughts as Rohan was only twenty-eight years old and hadn't had any children. I said to him that I would go and see if I could have my tubes untied so that we could have children together. At the same time panic started to develop about my age because I was starting to get closer to forty. We discussed it at length.

Rohan said, 'Look, if you can't have children, then I can't have children. It wouldn't matter to me, and I can help you raise Wayde as my own son.'

That's what type of guy he is. He is just adorable. My rock. However, I put all the negative thoughts aside, and was determined to try and give him a child. Anyway, I always yearned to have a little girl so I could brush her hair, buy her pretty outfits, and do girly stuff. The next week, and with no time to waste we went to see a Specialist to see if we could make it happen. The doctor advised it is possible, however, a total waste of time if Rohan is infertile. So off Rohan goes to do a fertility test, and his count was good. Phew!

I was immediately booked in for a tube reversal. Big operation. Huge. It was a four-hour operation, ten days in hospital. I had four drains coming out of my body and boy did they hurt coming out. I felt like they were dragging on every organ I had in my body. I was cut from hip to hip, I had the bent tubes cut out, and I had microsurgery to re-join the remainder. I did it. However, I loved Rohan deeply, and I would give anything to have a baby with this gorgeous man.

We planned this before we got married, as I was thirty-five then and worried about time running out as, I really didn't want any children after I had turned forty. During all this, we tried to keep our son Wayde, who was about thirteen and impressionable, informed of what was going on, and wanted to include him as much as possible.

For seven years it was just me and Wayde, and then Rohan came along, then we buy a house, and decide to get married. So big changes in a young boy's life, who still yearned for his biological father, understandably.

Wayde was a bit upset with us because he said to Rohan, 'You told me you were getting married, you didn't say you were having any children.'

I said to him, 'Wouldn't you like a little brother or sister to play with?'

He came around to the idea a bit after that and was excited to have a little brother. I don't think he was too keen on a sister though. I asked the doctor when we could start trying for a baby after the operation, he said as soon as you feel well enough, go ahead. Next month I was pregnant. Rohan and I were ecstatic. About three weeks later, I rang up the doctor and said I had started bleeding, he said it is a miscarry and because you are so early in your stage there is no need for a curette.

Another two weeks on from that, I was still bleeding. Not knowing how long I am supposed to bleed after a miscarriage, I rang the hospital, and asked them what the situation was, and what should I do. They told me I should ring my doctor straight away, as that is not normal. I rang my doctor and he said meet him at the Hospital. I had an ultrasound and he said it was in the tube. It didn't imbed in the womb. It is called an Ectopic pregnancy. I was put in Hospital to get the baby taken out of the tube. We were extremely disappointed and terribly upset, however, we had planned our wedding for the next year, September 1993, and had that to look forward to. We were both so upset and started to think maybe we can't have kids.

We decided to have our engagement party in Mackay, at our house. We invited seventy people, but I think there was more than that. We had friends come up from Melbourne, and various other places. Had an absolutely wonderful time, except Rohan decided to use dry ice to put at the bottom of an old fridge we used as an esky with normal ice on top. Turned out, it froze all the beers. We also had a visit from the police at about 3.00 am, politely asking us to turn the music down, and keep the noise down, as some neighbours a couple of blocks away complained. As we had our engagement in Mackay, Rohan thought it would be better if we got married in Melbourne because both Rohan's Nannas were too old to fly. It would also make it a bit cheaper as all his family was in Melbourne and I didn't have any family in Mackay.

We flew down to Melbourne September of the following year. As dad had passed away, we decided it would be awesome if my son Wayde gave me away. Rohan's mother planned a beautiful wedding down there for us, as we couldn't do much planning from Mackay. No internet then.

We got married in St. Agatha's Church in Cranbourne. Gorgeous reception. She did a really good job on the songs, a lot of them being Elvis songs. I loved Elvis. My dad used to sing Elvis songs to me. We were down there for a week, and then we came back as Mr. & Mrs. Howie. The following year I fell pregnant.

Living In Fear Of Enemies

So Lucky

I have a wonderful husband,
Wouldn't trade him in for quids.
I love him oh so dearly,
And our wonderful kids.

I feel so much at home with him,
I'd never marry again.
Now I've found my perfect match,
And give him a 10 out of 10.

He helps me so much with our kids,
No other could ever do.
They love him dearly just like me,
Our family love is true.

He comes home from work at night,
As tired as tired can be.
But always grabs the tea towel,
And has a cuddle for me.

I really feel so lucky,
To have this person in my life.
And also very happy,
He asked ME to be his wife.

Kathleen Howie

27. Growing Family

We went to the doctor's and found out everything was right with the second pregnancy. What a relief, however, there were still some anxious moments when things weren't right. We found out we were having a boy during the eighteen-week scan. Rohan was so excited as all fathers want their little man, and Wayde was excited to welcome a little brother. Deciding on a name for him was hard though because we wanted a special and unforgettable name for him.

We were all involved in the process, and Rohan came home from work one day with two names for me to think about: Trey or Teale. Rohan had seen a street name spelt Teal. I liked the sound of Teal, but I added an E on the end just to be different. Wayde wanted him to be called Jackson. So, we called him Teale Jackson Allen. Allen was Rohan's father's first name. I had Teale on the 15/1/1995.

Rohan's mum, Marie, came up a week before Teale was due, to help with the final few days of pregnancy, and assist with Teale after he was born. I was so grateful to have her there as it was a fifteen-hour labour, and she was most comforting, understanding, and supportive. Then Rohan's father, Allen, arrived the day after Teale was born. He rang the day before and asked how the weather was and we told him it has been very mild and not too hot. "BEAUTIFUL", we all said. The day he arrived had to be the hottest day we had had so far that summer, and the temperature jumped to thirty-two degrees, and the humidity was in the nineties. He thought we had falsely reported the weather to get him to Mackay.

The next day it was even hotter so Allen said we should go to the shopping centre, so he can sit in the air conditioning. Rohan was gob-smacked, as he explained to me that his dad hated shopping centres. Marie and I thought, great we can do some shopping and have a day out. We put Teale in the baby carrier, and Allen carried him around that shopping centre for three hours. We would go into shops, and he would sit on a bench, patiently waiting and proudly watching over his grandson.

Our room was next to Wayde's room, and our wardrobe was built along his bedroom wall. I knew Allen was a carpenter, so I mentioned to him if it was possible to build a wardrobe in Wayde's room, cutting a hole in the back of our wardrobe. He said, "No problems". Off he went, got the tools and materials, and proceeded to cut the wall at the back of our wardrobe.

I happened to be downstairs hanging out washing, and Allen came down with this long bit of steel rod.

He asked, 'What is this for?'

Living In Fear Of Enemies

My jaw dropped and said, 'Pop, that's a cyclone rod.'

Allen shrugged his shoulders and said, 'Oh well, hope you don't get a bad cyclone then.'

It was from an internal wall, so we thought it would be okay. The house is still standing to this day.

This was my first real introduction on how a loving family functions. I was amazed. This was all new to me, coming from a "chuck and shut" childhood.

After a while we decided that we wanted Teale to have a baby brother or sister, and Wayde loved his little brother, so much he thought another one wouldn't be so bad. I was still yearning for a little girl as well, so thought we would have one more crack. I now only have a couple of more years before I turn forty; time was running out.

Having another child now was still possible. Teale's first birthday was approaching, and we had struggled through on our own without any family assistance for a year now. It was a particularly hot summer, and Rohan suggested we should move to Melbourne to escape the heat, and to have some family support around.

28. Another Move

We decided to move down to Melbourne when Teale turned one year old. We wanted him to have more family around him like aunties, uncles, and cousins, as well as and most importantly, Nanna and Poppy. We also thought it would benefit Wayde, now fifteen, by having a strong family network. Rohan's mother and father doted on Wayde and treated him like their own grandson. My first thought was what the bloody hell am I doing going back to Melbourne. This was a place that chewed me up and spat me out last time, and I still had vivid memories of my checkered past there. This time, though, I was going there with a loving husband, two beautiful boys, and a family to support me. What could go wrong!

We bought a beautiful brick home with slate tile floors, pink carpet, ducted vacuum cleaner, and most importantly a heater. From our lounge and front lawn, we had a clear view of the city skyline. Well not long after we moved to Melbourne, I fall pregnant again. I had another miscarriage and was extremely upset and disappointed. Within six months of that happening, I fell pregnant again. This was another ectopic pregnancy. As this was the second one, it had damaged the tube, and I had to go to the hospital to have the tube removed. This setback left us with a feeling of emptiness and despair as time was running out. The odds were starting to stack up against me. I was now only left with one tube, and one more year to fall pregnant, if possible.

I thought my hopes for another child were ruined, as I only had one tube left, and the chances of falling pregnant again were slim to zero. My girlfriend was having a garage sale, so I decided to give her my cot, car seats, and other baby items for her to sell. Two weeks after these items were sold, I went to the doctor and found out I was pregnant again. Thinking to myself that it was probably in the tube, and that I had two ectopic pregnancies previously, I was going to lose it. I was telling Rohan not to get too excited, and he understood and felt the same. I was under a specialist and went in for scans straight away to determine if there were any issues.

I found out it was going to be a normal pregnancy, and that everything was situated correctly. Phew! Elated with the news, and full of joy I raced home, and told Rohan and the family, and waited for the eighteen-week scan, so I could see what sex it was going to be.

Could it possibly be a girl? Yeah right, don't get too excited. I was hoping so much for a girl. We both went in when it was time for me to have the scan. We could see the baby moving a bit and our eyes started searching for the signs of the baby's sex. You could see the legs were crossed and not moving.

Dejectedly the doctor said, 'It is not going to show

us what sex it is today.' As he was about to complete the scan and the last possible moment, the baby's legs parted and he excitedly said, 'It is a girl.'

I said, 'Are you sure?'

He confirmed the sex, and tears started streaming down my cheeks, and I looked up at Rohan, and tears were streaming down his cheeks as well, and he hugged me tightly. We cried all the way home, and it has been one of the happiest moments of my life.

Once the joy subsided of having a girl, the pain of childbirth overcame me, and I was having terrible nightmares over Wayde and Teale's births. It was a hard and traumatic experience. Wayde wasn't too bad he took about two hours to appear, however, still painful. Teale however was fifteen hours of excruciating pain, and worse was to come as I still had to push him out. It's all fun and exciting when you are pregnant, and you are eagerly awaiting to welcome your child into the world, but then you realise it has to come out. OMG! I had to let my doctor know of these nightmares and being terrified of this upcoming birth. I begged him can I please have a caesarean.

He said, 'Yes, you want a caesarean, you can have a caesarean,'

It was a safer option especially at my age. What a relief I was so happy to hear that.

Our little girl was born on 19/8/1997. We named her Maddison Tayla Marie Howie. Marie is Rohan's mother's first name. As I was turning forty the following February, we decided to have the last tube tied when I had the caesarean.

It was all so exciting, and I could finally hold my daughter. We took her home. The boys were eagerly awaiting her arrival at home, especially Teale. We were giving him little nurses of his sister.

As he handed her back to me, he said, 'She is so lovely, mummy, you can take her back to Dandenong Hospital now.'

Laughing internally, I said, 'No, she is here for good.'

Teale gave me a bit of a somewhat perplexed and concerned look. Maddison started crying a bit.

Teale then said, 'Please take her back to Dandenong Hospital'.

Moving to Melbourne was where I realised what being in a family meant. Having Rohan's parents nearby, lovingly helping with family matters, babysitting, and raising our children. I affectionately called his dad Allen. Pop, and his mum, Marie, Nan. Nothing was ever a problem and when we needed them, they were there.

Two weeks prior to us moving to Melbourne, we needed to send Wayde down to get settled and start school. Nan and Pop took him in and accepted him as their first grandson and treated him as family. They enrolled him in school, got his uniforms and drove him there every day.

One day we had our water pipes on the dishwasher burst, spewing hot water all over our beautiful slate flooring, and I could hear the tiles pop.

I immediately rang Pop and screamed on the phone 'Help me, the water pipes have burst. Water is going everywhere. Near the carpet in the lounge. What do I do?'

Pop said, 'Go out the front and turn off the water.'

I am frantically running around trying to find this mains water tap. How naïve I was those days. Well, Nan and Pop were there within minutes carrying mops, buckets and other cleaning items, and swiftly went into action.

Pop was a carpenter, and we had a few renovations at our house we needed done. We mentioned one day to Pop that we would like a nice carport along the side of the house, a sandpit, and a little patio area with a bench seat to watch the kids in the backyard playing in the sandpit. Well, off he goes that day to the timberyard, and hardware store and gets all the materials. The next day he turns up early, and he is in action starting all the projects. This was highly unusual for me as I never had anyone do things like this for me.

The only time he got angry was when I tried to return some of his kindness, by hosing out his back patio, cleaning windows and clearing out all the cobwebs, whilst Nan and Pop were shopping.

I thought to myself, Nan and Pop will love this, and I was so proud and felt I was important.

Well, Pop walked in and said, 'Who the hell has used all this water? We are on water restrictions.'

My smile turned to a look of shock, and I said, 'Oops, sorry, Pop, it was me. I was just trying to surprise you with a nice clean patio.'

I was then expecting punishment.

Pop said jokingly, 'Well, I am going have a nice clean bill now.'

He never stayed mad, and it ended up the joke of the week, and funny family story.

Pop was a man of few words and did all his talking through his actions. I had a really close connection with Pop, and he was like a second father to me, and he treated me like his own daughter. He never judged me. He never criticised me. He just loved and supported me. Pop later died from a heart attack, and due to me suffering vertigo, I couldn't attend his funeral, so I penned this poem to capture what he meant to me.

She'll be Right, Mate!

Awoken again at four in the morn,
Feeling sadness in the air,
A great family member,
Is now not there,

As a new day starts without Big Al,
I'm remembering back on his life,
When I met him, He had three beautiful children?
And a fantastic wife,

I married one of his children,
Rohan is his name,
But put a nail and hammer in his hands,
And no, he's not the same,

Visiting us in Brisbane,
I always found him a chore,
Teale had got his head stuck,
Between the fridge and the drawer,

Alan had an idea,
To just cut out the drawer,
It looked so fine and dandy,
But now look at the floor,

He would never leave things messy,
So off he goes again,
He bought the tiles,
Laid them down,
I gave him ten out of ten,

I was never used to this treatment,
Family doing things for me,
He opened up my eyes,
To what a family is supposed to be,

Came to visit in Mackay,
Seventeen years ago,
Built a cupboard in a room,
Thought this piece of steel must go,

Bought it out into the laundry,
To make sure everything was right,
I said, 'Pop, it's a cyclone rod!'
And couldn't stop laughing all night,

He definitely was a champion,
That's all I have to say,
He always seemed so relaxed,
In his own little way,

He's looking down on us right now,
Seeing the sadness of his fate,
He'd lift his shoulder and his eyebrow,
And say, 'She'll be right, mate!'

Proud to take your name,
Loving daughter-in-law,

Kathy.

29. Bad Luck Returns

About six months later, I caught this really bad flu. I was awake most of the night coughing. I went to the doctors the next morning and asked him to give me something to stop my coughing. He wouldn't give me any antibiotics, but he gave me a mild cough mixture that did nothing. For the next two days I was so sick and up all night coughing. I coughed that hard I couldn't breathe in deep. My chest was so sore, and it was really hard to walk.

I went back to the same doctor, and he checked me out, and pressed my ribs. I screamed so loud. He told me I had a broken rib. I mentioned all of my broken bones, which was four by then, and not realising it was actually five. He sent me for a Bone Density Test. The results were that I had severe Osteoporosis. He told me to take a certain type of Calcium tablet. However, when I went to buy some, they were far too big, and I can't swallow large tablets. I wiped it off and thought that I will just drink a lot of milk instead. I know, stupid of me. You should really do what the doctor says.

Years later when I was living in Brisbane, I had a chest x-ray and they found that there was two old broken ribs, not one as the doctor in Melbourne had thought. No wonder I was so sore. I had broken them from all the coughing I had been doing.

When Maddie was about six months old, I decided to go back to work. Maddie was bottle fed, and Teale was about two years old. I decided to go back to work at night as Rohan worked during the day. Same as we did in Mackay. I got a job as a bar attendant at a nice-looking establishment close to where we lived. I would have the kid's bathed and ready for bed. Rohan would come home, and I would have all the dinner ready, and I would head off to work behind the bar. Once again, we seemed like ships in the night passing each other for about half an hour.

One particular night, I had started closing up the public bar when about ten people decided to turn up, very drunk and boisterous. It was a busload of people from Yallourn, on their way home from a trip to the casino in Melbourne. They were trying to get into the public bar, and I told the bouncer no, they couldn't come in here as we were closing. He decided to send them in to the gaming area, where the Poker machines were. I just finished closing down the TAB when I heard one hell of a commotion from the gaming area. I ran in and it was like a blood bath. Bodies flying everywhere, a bouncer's head got shoved through a poker machine. There were girls fighting, men fighting, yelling, and screaming.

There was a customer sitting up at the bar called, Little Pat. He was so drunk he could hardly stand.

He was yelling at me, 'Kathy, get a glass of ice.'

I got him a glass of ice and I passed it to him, and Pat shoved this thing into it which I thought was a piece of raw meat.

I screamed 'What the hell is that?'

He yelled 'It is Gary's ear.'

I screamed again 'What do you mean, it is Gary's ear?'

Gary was another regular patron. I looked over and Gary's face was full of blood. Pat said to me this bloke had bitten Gary's ear off and spat it on the floor.

Pat drunkenly said, 'I am trying to preserve it, so stick some more ice on the top of it.'

I started instantly dry reaching and gagging once it hit me what was going on.

I just screamed at Pat, 'Get the bloody glass out of my hand.'

I had my arm extended and my head facing the other way so I couldn't see the ear in the glass.

He couldn't reach so I screamed again, 'Get around in the bar and get this thing out of my hand now.'

I was so sick. I didn't eat meat for the next year. I

literally became a vegetarian. While this was unfolding, the fight continued and ended up spilling out into the hallway. My supervisor, who was a female, was thrown by this girl up against a cement pot almost knocking her out. I was in full panic mode now, and I was so scared someone was going to get seriously hurt. I was thinking what I could do to stop this fight.

I started screaming out, 'The police are here, the police are here.'

They all scattered out of the hotel. I don't know where they went however, I assume they jumped in their bus and took off. The police arrived and began taking statements and eyewitness accounts. The police did manage to detain two of the offenders as they were escaping.

Once things had calmed down and we helped with injured patrons and staff, we commenced the clean-up and assess the damage. I scanned the bar area in gaming, and there was blood everywhere on the bar, on the stools and floor, so I started cleaning up. I wanted to wipe everything down, so I removed the bar mats and was squeezing them out into the sink and quickly realised they were full of blood. This was around the period when AIDS was a huge concern, and I was a bit worried as I had cut myself on the dishwasher earlier that night.

I told my supervisor, and she said I had to get tested for AIDS and Hepatitis. It was a nervous time, as I had to be tested every three months for a whole year. I am so lucky that all of the tests came back clear. Gary ended up with a pixie ear. It was half gone, and it could not be sown back on. After all that ear in the ice business, and making me very sick, it was to no avail.

Another incident that happened at that hotel. This young guy had come up to the bar and asked one of our regulars for a lend of their lighter. He then raced off out of the bar with it. Next day we had the Police come in asking about a guy who had pinched a lighter. We obliged the police with his details. Subsequently he was arrested and put in jail. It became apparent that the previous night, when he stole the lighter, he went and set fire to a radiology and x-ray practice. Millions of dollars went up in flames. I had to go to the Police Station and make a statement again.

I said to the Police Officer, 'Am I working at the roughest hotel in Melbourne?'

He said, 'No, the second roughest pub. There is a Pub in Dandenong that is the roughest.'

This was how rough the pub was; one of our regulars was known to keep machetes in his ute out the front. What for, I never found out nor wanted to find out for that matter. Luckily, he liked me, I was his favourite barmaid. I knew I was safe when he was there, and no one would hurt me. We often found needles in the toilets, and there were regular fights and dust ups. I was starting to get fed up with the constant incidents, and police visits at the hotel, and sick of the miserable weather.

It was so cold, wet and miserable in Melbourne, and depressing and after living there for three years,

I had had enough. I had indents in my ankles from my socks and my skin hadn't been touched by the sun for a long time. I lived in socks twenty-four hours a day, literally. I yearned for the sun, tropical breezes, and the warmth of Queensland again. I asked Rohan to please try and get a transfer back to Mackay. I loved the family environment in Melbourne, but I really wanted to go back to Queensland.

Rohan was eventually offered a position in Brisbane with a different company. So in 1999, the closest we could get to Mackay was Brisbane. We thought this was a good compromise, because I was back in Queensland, and Brisbane was halfway between his family in Melbourne, and my hometown of Mackay. So off we went to Brisbane.

It seems every time something goes bad in my life, I have to move on.

30. Back to Queensland

We travelled to Brisbane one weekend to look at potential homes, and we were assisted by a friend in real estate, so he had plenty for us to look at when we got there. We settled on this beautiful two storey house with a beautiful in-ground pool. It had a playroom for the kids, a spare room downstairs, with an ensuite, and an excellent outdoor entertaining area. Our new house was in a very quiet, dead end street and leafy suburb. It wasn't Mackay, but at least it was warmer and sunnier than Melbourne.

Maddi was only two years old, and Teale started Kindergarten there. Everything seemed to be going really well, and we were very happy once again. I got work immediately at a local tavern, and Rohan got stuck into his new job. Rohan loved his AFL, and became a member of the Brisbane Lions, and the kids got into swimming, and other activities. We also made regular treks to the Gold Coast beaches.

I recalled from years prior to the move, that my brother Barry lived in Brisbane. Albeit twenty years beforehand. I looked up the phone book and I found his daughter, Dianne. I explained to her that I was Barry's sister, and I hadn't seen him for many years. I am your Aunty Kathy. I hadn't seen Dianne since she was about four years old. She was about twenty-five now. She gave me Barry's address. I packed Rohan and the kids up one Saturday morning, and we went to his place.

I stood in the doorway and nervously knocked on the door, not knowing what to expect, after all it had been twenty years since I had seen him. He opened the door, not expecting us, and I really thought that he thought we were some kind of door knockers or salespeople.

I said to him, 'Barry, do you remember me?'

He looked at me blankly and said. 'No, should I?'

I was a bit surprised and said. 'Yes, I am your sister, Kathy.'

Well his mouth just dropped, and he was in disbelief.

He kept saying 'Kathy? Kathy?'

I said 'Yes, Kathy Wessel.'

Barry said, 'Oh, come in, come in.'

He made us a lovely cup of coffee, and we caught up on things we had been doing. He met Teale and Maddi for the first time. It was so lovely to see him after all this time. Me not being very family orientated, I didn't

Living In Fear Of Enemies

want to live on his doorstep, but it was nice to see him occasionally. I invited him around for a family BBQ, and to my surprise he turned up.

I told him he was my hero when we were young. How his rebellious and cheeky teenage years gave me joy. He was shocked. To not have my big brother around to protect me was extremely saddening, and it was a real shame how our family was separated all those years ago. I am the type now to probably not see him for another five, ten or twenty years, as I was never used to having that family support around me in my younger days. To some people that would probably seem odd. I guess I can attribute this to the way I was raised, and that I was always on my own. You didn't need me then, so why need me now.

Our move to Brisbane was just at the turn of the century. The year 2000. New year, new century, new start, new life. I get a phone call out of the blue from this lady, and to my surprise she stated that I was her Aunty. She expressed to me that her name was Kathleen, and that she was named after me. Apparently, she was Barry's daughter, who he had adopted out, and totally unbeknown to me. She advised that she lived on the Sunshine Coast, and would love to meet with me.

Hold on, wait a minute.

At one stage I had little or no family, and now all of a sudden, I had family members coming out of the woodwork. The thought of new family members excited me, however, it was also met with trepidation, as I had been discarded by so called family over the years. We decided to go and visit her. She turned out to be such a lovely person, and we spent the whole day with her. She helped fill a few missing gaps in my family history.

Rohan's Nanna, Jean, came up from Melbourne for holidays. She was eighty-two years old, and often travelled to different places on her own. We decided to take Nanna and the kids into South Bank, which is a popular and beautiful tourist attraction of Brisbane city. There is a manmade beach there, and always has live entertainment, markets and street performers. On this particular day, there was guy on a unicycle, juggling, jumping on beer cartons with his unicycle, and spinning around. The kids wanted to stay and watch, so we found a spot close to the performance area. I decided to stay further back with Nan, and Rohan was halfway to the stage keeping an eye on the kids.

I said to Rohan, 'Are the kids with you, make sure the kids are alright.'

He turned and said, 'They are fine, they are up the front watching the show.'

At that time, Maddi was three, and Teale was five. He loved his kids but sometimes he was a bit to nonchalant and unaware of potential dangers. However, I was the opposite, and my senses were always raised given my experiences.

I said, 'No, I will look after them, you come back and look after your Nanna.'

I went up the front to look after the kids. Maddi was more excited about the rocks around the bottom of the palm trees, so she sat closer to the rocks, and I stood really close to her, with Teale on the other side. Teale was transfixed on the performance. Back and forth from watching the show to watching her. I took a look at her playing with rocks. I then looked up at the show and then back at her. In what seemed like a split second of taking my eyes off her I looked down, and she was gone. I quickly scanned the immediate vicinity with no sign of her.

I stopped the show by screaming at the top of my voice, 'Maddi, Maddi, where are you? I can't find my daughter.'

There were thousands of people there. I was trying to look down through their legs to see if I could find her to no avail. I was screaming. I grabbed Teale and ran to Rohan. He saw the look of fear in my face and said what's wrong.

I screamed, 'I can't find Maddi.'

I asked Teale to stand still with Nanna and don't move. Rohan and I were both frantically screaming at the top of our voices. We went down to the manmade beach first, because we knew she couldn't swim, and it was just full of people. There were lifeguards, and we hurriedly ran to them screaming. They were madly on their two ways putting a watch alert out for a little blue-eyed, blonde-haired girl in a blue dress.

While they were doing that, I went one way and Rohan went the other, yelling out to Maddi, eyes darting around and scanning the crowd for her. It was like all the blood was running from my body. My little girl is gone. It's a very strange feeling, because one part of you tries to convince you to relax it will be okay, you will find her. The other part of you is just utter devastation, and the horrible realisation that you will never see your daughter again.

It seemed like forever but was probably only ten to fifteen minutes. We were frantically searching for her, heads swivelling, scanning the crowd again, with the lifeguards, and calling out her name.

This lady approached us, with a little girl in her arms and said, 'Is this the girl your looking for?'

We were so focused on finding Maddi, that we looked straight passed her, and didn't even comprehend that the lady was holding Maddi in her arms. We grabbed Maddi, and just held her in our arms, tightly, with tears streaming down our faces. This wonderful good Samaritan said Maddi was nearly out near the road, which was a long way from where we were watching the show. The lady said she was crying and calling, mummy, mummy, mummy. We think Maddi must have looked up and then looked to her left and thought Mummy had gone and tried to find me. If she had looked too her right, she would have seen I was standing right next to her.

That wonderful lady who found her, I didn't even get to thank her properly. I was in so much of a panic initially, and then euphoria overwhelmed me, that I just blanked her out, and my focus was entirely on Maddi. I am sure we thanked her, but not nearly enough. I didn't want to stay at South bank any longer. I just wanted to get my daughter home safely, so we packed up and went home immediately. I just slumped in my seat with shear exhaustion and utter relief. I don't think I took my eyes off Maddi for the rest of day, and checked on her during the night.

31. The Stabbing

I worked at Aussie's Beenleigh Tavern, which was about twenty minute's drive from home, as a bar and gaming attendant. The tavern had a sports/public bar, bottle shop; Pete's Bar, which was the lounge and Bistro; The Rum Room, which was a function room, and adjoining the tavern was Crystals night club. I worked with some wonderful people there, and a friendly resident ghost named Boson. My understanding is that Boson worked in the original Tavern that included a rum distillery. Boson covertly ran a secret pipe and tap from the tavern to his house to steal rum. He was eventually caught and was hung in the hotel. So, the story goes. I feel he existed, as I would often be at work and doing the close-down process, which included turning off all the TAB TV screens.

I would then sit down with another staff member and wait for our supervisor to lock up the office, and then we would leave. As we were sitting there talking, all the TV's would suddenly come back on, and we would sit there in disbelief. Boson would also often lock doors to certain rooms, so you always had to carry a set of keys.

After a while, it became a game with Boson, and we got used to him. Boson came to us as pink balloon one night. Again, sitting there at knock off time waiting for the supervisor, this pink balloon travelled horizontally in front of us. The balloon was getting higher and headed towards a doorway.

I then said, 'Hey, Boson, you are going to hit your head if you don't duck.'

At that moment, the balloon quickly lowered and travelled through the doorway to the next bar. My co-worker and I sat there, astonished with goosebumps and eyes and jaws wide open. From where we were sitting, we could see the balloon disappear behind the bar in the other room.

I said, 'Oh, not playing anymore? You chicken.'

In the very next moment, the balloon reappeared above the bar, motionless. Once again, our eyes and mouths were agape. The balloon then disappeared again, and when the supervisor arrived, we told her, and went looking for the balloon. To our amazement, we could not find it. I later found out that balloons never travel horizontally or travel up and down. If they have helium, they will only go up, and if they have a hole, they will only go down.

Our uniforms were a bright yellow shirt and black skirts or pants. There was one particular co-worker, Sandra. She had a wonderful personality, and she would often confide in me about her personal life. Of course, I felt like I had a connection to her, given my history, and felt she needed a friend. I always seemed to connect with people that have suffered fractured lives. Sandra had explained to me that she had an estranged husband, who had verbally and physically abused her for years. This animal would beat her, and threaten to kill her, and on one occasion, urinated on her while she was on the ground after a beating, and suffering with broken ribs. She would often arrive at work with bruises and soreness that she endeavoured to cover with makeup, and as battered wives do. she had some lame excuses for the injuries. He had placed a nude photo of her in the men's toilets at the tavern with her phone number in order to humiliate her. This was the type of disgusting abuse this asshole would inflict on her.

Sandra had finally decided, for her own safety, to leave her home and had to make the difficult decision to leave her children behind, some as young as five and seven. He had threatened to harm them, as well, if she took them. Sandra was living in an undisclosed location, and the husband did not have her contact details. Sandra would catch the train to work to avoid detection. Her husband would often contact work to see if she was there. After many threating incidents, and in discussions with management, it was decided that it was too dangerous for her and the staff, if she remained working at the tavern. Sandra decided she should move on and she was due to finish up a week later.

On 2nd February 2001, I had prepared dinner for my family and waited for Rohan to arrive home. As usual, he would come up stairs and give us all a hug. We would exchange pleasantries, and a quick catch up of the day, a couple of kisses and off to work I went. My shift commenced at six pm, in the sports bar. At approximately seven pm, Sandra came rushing in from

Pete's bar and lounge, and advised me that her husband had asked one of her kids to ring mum's work and see if she was there.

Another worker, Natalie, answered the phone and without thinking and said, 'Oh yeah, mum's here.'

Sandra just had this look of absolute terror and panic on her face, as she raced in to tell me in the sports bar. I told her to come and sit in the sports bar when she had finished her shift and I would run her to the train station. She went back to Pete's Bar to continue to serve meals, with about thirty customers waiting to be served. At roughly around seven-thirty pm, blood curdling screams erupted from Pete's Bar. I rushed in to see what was going on, and the supervisor howled at me to ring the police. I grabbed the phone and dialled 000, still unaware of what was going on. At the same time, another employee dashed off to get security.

The police where asking me all these questions; however, I was still unaware of what had happened, and quickly handed the phone to the supervisor, and continued into Pete's Bar. There I found Sandra just standing there, holding on to the bar with a look of despair, and a small cut on her face.

I screamed 'My god, he got you, didn't he?'

At that point her eyes rolled back, and she began to go faint and collapse. I quickly moved in and grabbed her by the waist, and another worker grabbed her head and shoulders and we laid her on the ground. Blood began seeping through the bright yellow shirt in a few spots and it soon became apparent that he had stabbed her a few times.

We later discovered that once her husband realised, she was at work he decided to act. He grabbed a carving knife from home and came to the tavern to exact revenge. He casually walked into Pete's Bar, concealing the knife and no-one even noticed his presence. He just strolled behind the bar, eyes fixed on Sandra, and stabbed her four or five times, quickly turned, and ran straight out. It all happened so fast that a lot of staff and patrons didn't even see it occur. Luckily a couple of patrons and security saw him run off, and chased him outside where he slipped over, and they grabbed him until police arrived.

The ambulance soon arrived and began treating Sandra. I just went into panic mode, unaware of what to do, and ran back to my bar knowing customers were still waiting to be served. I attempted to serve a patron a Vodka and ice, but just spilt it everywhere, as I couldn't control my shaking. A fellow worker noticed what state I was in, and took over, and advised me to go and sit down. I don't know why, but I decided the best place for me was with Sandra, so I went back into Pete's Bar, and sat beside her rubbing her legs while the ambulance crew worked frantically to stabilise her.

She was bleeding profusely, and then a male ambulance worker said he can't remove her bra until a female ambulance worker or police officer arrived.

I said, 'Just give me the god damn scissors and I will cut it off.'

Once they stabilised her, they transported her to the ambulance, and they said we need someone to go with her.

The supervisor said, 'Kathy, you go.'

Why me?, I thought, but then I felt I could comfort her, and talk to her in the ambulance, so she knew there was a friend there, and a familiar voice. I was sitting in the front seat of the ambulance waiting to go, talking to Sandra, and telling her to hang on.

As we were about to go, the ambulance workers in the back yelled, 'Not yet, her blood pressure is dropping rapidly, and we need to stabilise her.'

They were going to take her to the Logan Hospital, however they decided to head to the Princess Alexandra Hospital, as they felt she was in a far more serious condition than first thought. It was at that point that I had this frightful feeling that she was going to die in the ambulance, and we would arrive at the hospital, and they would declare her D.O.A. I advised the driver that I couldn't go with them.

He said, 'Well hurry up, and make up your mind, because when they say go, we are off.'

I clambered out of the ambulance, and collapsed in the gutter, overwhelmed by guilt that I couldn't be with Sandra, and console her and that I had let her down. I just sobbed and sobbed with my head on my knees as I sat in the gutter. The other part of the guilt was that I should have said something to the supervisor immediately Sandra advised me her husband had contacted the tavern. Maybe they would have sent her home.

I did mention this to the supervisor, and she said that they felt Sandra would be safer if she had stayed at work, and that no-one would be able to get her there. Thankfully, Sandra survived this heinous act, however, she was in a medically induced coma for three days with four severe stab wounds. I, however, suffered some trauma and nightmares for a few weeks, as I kept visualising the awful sight of Sandra's expression on her face before she collapsed, and the blood seeping through the bright yellow shirt. Her estranged husband got eight years in jail. I know, right, unbelievable!

32. The Armed Robbery

It seemed like I had only just, got back to some normality in my life, and the visions of the stabbing had faded, when fate dealt me another blow. It was Monday the 4th of February, 2002, and again I hug and kiss my family goodbye, and head off to work at the tavern.

My shift commenced at six pm, as usual. It was about seven-thirty pm, and I was assisting a new worker, Brett, with TAB reporting, and how to print out all the reports. I then explained to him the reason for this was that there had been a lot of robberies in the area, and this allows the TAB staff to see what transactions had been processed that day, and total monies taken. I then worked my shift until ten-thirty pm, which was closing time for the gaming, bar and TAB, and the tavern was locked up. Lily, a fellow employee, and I were in the process of clearing out all the poker machines of the takings for the day. We would place the money in individual bags for each machine. Another fellow employee, Damien, came in from the bottle shop after closing, and was ready to go home. One of us would walk Damien to the door, unlock it, and let him out, and then lock up again. On this occasion, I asked Lily if she could let Damien out, as I had a couple more poker machines to clear. I don't think Lily minded, as I had bored her all night, constantly talking about my daughters first day of Pre School, and how I was going to do her hair, dress her, and how excited I was. Lily grabbed the keys and walked Damien to the door. I blissfully kept clearing machines, with thoughts running through my head of my daughter's first day at Pre School the next morning, and how I would dress her and do her hair.

I then hear Damien yelling out to me.

I just casually walked towards him and asked, 'What's the matter?'

I saw this guy behind Damien, and Damien said, 'You need to get on the floor.'

I just dismissed it thinking it was him and his mates mucking around. I turned to go back to work.

I hear Damien again in much deeper and terrified voice, 'Get down on the floor, Kathy.'

I turned around, and that's when the gravity of the whole situation hit me. There was Damien, laying on the ground with a man standing over him wearing a balaclava, and pointing a gun to his head. I had no idea where Lily was, but later discovered she was curled up in an eating booth crying and screaming.

Sheer terror enveloped me, and all I could think of was how much my life was in danger, with no concern for the other workers. Your mind and body then goes into self-preservation mode, and you either fight or flight. I took off and ran back into gaming, grabbed all the bags of poker machine money, and ran past the TAB area, and stashed it under the counter and continued to run.

I could hear a deep gravelly voice say, 'Where is she going? Get her.'

I look back and it still astonished me that I prioritised the tavern's money over my own life, and other employees, and I still cannot fathom why that was my instant thought in that moment. The tavern had put us through some training in the event there was any type of robbery, and the trainers always say comply with the robbers. I can tell you now, all training goes out the window, and your instincts take over, and you just react. Maybe I reacted that way due to my history, I was always trying to escape horrible situations. It still makes me feel sick in the stomach today, and I am not sure I could trust myself if I found myself in the same situation, training or not.

I kept running, dodging kegs of beer, leaping over pallets, never looking back, eyes darting around looking for a way out. All the time I could hear the robbers yelling, "Get her". Fear kept driving me forward, and I felt I was going to die any minute and expecting to hear a gun go off. Images of my daughter going to pre-school started flooding my mind, and I thought I would never get to see her again. I made it to the loading dock, ducking and weaving pallets of beer, empty boxes, kegs, and other items, never looking back. No way out.

I knew the main office was close, which we called

the Dungeon, as it was tucked away in a dark corner of the tavern. The shift supervisor, Denise, was working in there doing paperwork, and placing the days takings in the safe.

I started yelling out, 'Denise! Denise! Open the door.'

I was so terrified that she would have the door locked, as she was handling money. The door was open, thank God, and hope overcame fear, and I thought to get in there and lock the door. Safe. I see Denise standing outside the Dungeon, with a startled look on her face, and I reach her, breathless, lungs burning and legs aching.

I managed to get out, 'We're getting robbed. We're getting robbed!'

We quickly ran into the Dungeon, and Denise closed the door behind us, locked it and turned off the lights. We remained quiet and hoped that the robbers would think I had hidden somewhere or escaped.

Denise looked through a peephole in the door, and observed a man walk past the door, and then back again. It appeared he had lost me, and some relief started to enter my mind. Denise turned on the lights, and I picked up the phone, and tried to dial 000 but I was shaking far too much to even dial the numbers.

I said to Denise, 'We need to ring the police.'

However, she was in state of disbelief and couldn't

really fathom what was going on.

It was then we heard Damien's frightened voice, 'Denise, open the door. Denise, you have got to open the door.'

Denise looked out the peephole and saw that the robbers had a gun to Damien's head.

She turned back to me hesitantly, and said, 'Put the phone down, we have to open the door.'

I was shaking my head no, however, the tone of her voice indicated that it was serious, so I reluctantly put the phone down. Denise slowly unlocked and then opened the door.

The robbers yelled furiously 'Put your hands up, and your heads down. Do not look at us!'

As thoughts of my daughter flashed through my mind, I begged to them, 'Please don't hurt us, we have families.'

One of the robbers marched us into the next room, which was the old staffroom. He marshalled the four of us towards the round table in the room and directed us to sit down. Whilst he watched over us, the other robbers were clearing out the Dungeon and other areas of the tavern. I managed to sneak a look and the man watching us had a balaclava on, however, I will never forget his piercing blue eyes and bushy red eyebrows, and the smell of stale beer on his breath. He asked if we were the only staff on, and we confirmed that.

Kathy Howie

At that point, I thought he was going to shoot us all, as he was constantly fiddling with the back of his belt. I can only assume that was where he had his gun. We were sitting around this table, heads down, trembling, and fearful of what was going to happen next. He advised us to just calm down, and if we didn't do anything stupid, then no one would get hurt. I thought of my actions earlier and how selfish I was to put everyone at risk, however, as I explained, self-preservation kicks in, and you only have thoughts of survival.

I then realised I had keys in my hand which would give them access to every poker machine and till draw. Immediately, I thought if he finds these keys, he will think I have deliberately kept them from him. So, what do I do, I slowly tuck them under my leg and endeavour to hide the keys. Idiot!

The guy guarding us in the room sensed we were scared, and he asked us, 'Is there anything I can get for you?'

I am imaging this is our last rights, so I said, 'A smoke would be nice.'

He then proceeded to hand us all a smoke. Then the weirdest thing happened, he started to massage Damien's shoulders to try and relax him. He then started telling us that he was a family man and had four children at home and did this for a living.

After what seemed like an eternity, but was probably only minutes, we heard one of his accomplices yell out, 'Right. We have got to go.'

The man watching over us in the staffroom then advised us to leave it for ten minutes before notifying the police, as they had police scanners and they would know if we did it earlier. He also said if we do notify them earlier, he would know, and there would be retribution. He then exited the room, and all went quiet. We sat in that room quietly trembling and listening for any noises. We waited for what we thought was ten minutes. We then huddled together holding hands and made our way to the Dungeon where Denise called 000 and the tavern manager, Julia.

I then felt like we had to ensure we were locked in, and that no-one else could get in. Denise was on the phone, and Lily was curled up crying.

I said to Damien, 'We need to lock the front door, and check the others.'

Damien was visibly shaking and didn't want to go, and I could tell in his eyes he was terrified, as was I, but I didn't feel safe until I knew all the doors were locked. I grabbed Damien's hand, both of us shaking, terrified that they may still be there watching us. We ducked down slightly walking slowly, and peeking around every corner, and made our way to the front door. When I felt we were close enough I sprinted to the door and locked it and let out a huge sigh of relief. I looked back at Damien who had slumped to the ground, head on his knees.

I said, 'We're alive, Damien. We're alive.'

I think then I was just overwhelmed with emotions,

and I too slumped to the ground, and started sobbing, and again images of my daughter entered my mind. The police arrived, and soon after, Julia, the manager. We told the police what had happened, and then we had to go to the police station to give statements. They asked Damien why he let them in, and he advised that the guy that came to the door was wearing a suit and tie, and showed him a police badge, and said he was from Jimboomba Police.

It was about two am, and the Human Resources manager for the company that owned the tavern asked if I wanted him to let my husband know, and that I may be late. I said no, I will ring him and tell him as I didn't want him to be too alarmed. I called Rohan and just said there had been some trouble at the tavern, and they just needed a statement from me, and I would be home soon. He was used to me doing police statements, so he didn't think too much of it, and went back to bed. It was about three-thirty am before the police finished with us. The Human Resources Manager escorted me home.

We arrived home. I opened the door, and my husband was standing at the top of the stairs. I entered, and then the HR Manager entered.

Rohan said, 'What's going on?'

You could imagine the look on Rohan's face when his wife turns up with a strange man at four am. The HR Manager quickly explained what had happened, and I could see his perplexed expression change to one of shock, anger, and then sadness. He just hugged and kissed me and tried to comfort me.

I didn't sleep at all that night. When the kids got up that morning. I just hugged them so hard and kissed them. I did get to see my daughter's first day of pre-school, although I don't really remember it. My husband had to do her hair, so he put her in cute little pig tails. I looked at photos later on and noticed that the part in her hair was like a jagged piece of lightning. My husband tried so hard to make our daughter look cute on her first day, and all I could see was the crooked part. Made me so sad.

We tried to keep it from the children, however, our son Teale, who was six at the time, was a very gifted young boy, and could read at a high school level. The next day, the local paper had been delivered and there was an article about the robbery.

We don't know why, but Teale read the article and asked, 'Mummy that's where you work.'

We just brushed it off, but he knew I worked at that tavern, and that I was at work that night.

I couldn't go back to work, and I descended into a deep depression, later diagnosed as Post Traumatic Stress Disorder (PTSD). I wouldn't leave the house or go to places where I felt there could be a robbery. We got invited to BBQs and parties, and we would all get ready but when it came time to leave, I just froze and said, "No, I can't go". It was so disappointing for Rohan and the kids.

I would retreat to my room, or to our office downstairs, and lock the door. Rohan would often come home from work and find me in the office with tears running down my cheeks. He was my rock, he tried to keep things as normal as possible for the kids, and did as much with them as possible, even if I couldn't go. I don't think he really knew what to do, or fully understood what I was going through. He was trying to do things he thought would help me, asking me how I was feeling, but I was starting to shut him out as well. I tried to push myself to do things but fear just consumed me, and I didn't want to leave the safety of our home.

I remember one time, sitting in the office with the door locked just playing mind numbing games on the computer, when there was a knock at the door. It was Maddison, my daughter.

She said, 'Mummy, I have drawn a picture for you. Can I show you?'

I didn't answer her.

She said, 'Please, mummy, can I show you?'

I didn't answer again. Then there was silence, and this piece of paper appeared under the door, and it was her picture. I just burst into tears, but still didn't open the door. That still hurts today. I started writing poetry in my solace, and this helped me to slowly heal. I was taking Valium, prescribed by a doctor, and was starting to descend into an even deeper depressed state, thinking my life was just shit, and maybe I am better off not being here.

Suicidal thoughts had entered my mind again.

Living In Fear Of Enemies

What turned me around was one day I was feeling down, and my daughter came up beside me, and just held my hand. I looked down, and she just gave me this huge loving smile. No words were spoken. That one simple touch and moment stays with me to this day. The instant warmth of that gesture made me realise that my children are my purpose in life. I never had my mother to guide me, and I wasn't going to do that to my children.

The warmth of a hand

Walking with my family,
Always hand in hand.
Never thought too much of it,
But now I understand.

When you hold another hand,
The warmth does come within.
Just concentrate and you will feel,
The love just flowing in.

You know its coming from the heart,
And generating yours,
Makes you feel so beautiful,
And opens up some doors.

So, when you're walking with your kin,
Try this touch of love.
It really works, it really does,
The warmth is like a glove.

Kathleen Howie

I often wonder why PTSD had never struck me before, with all the awful things in my life. I feel the robbery was the final straw, and all the horrible things that had happened in my life had just mounted up, and it all spilled over after the robbery. We were offered therapy sessions, and Denise and I decided to attend them. I needed to do something to understand how to get through this PTSD. They decided to take us back to the tavern, to revisit the scene of the crime. This made me feel extremely anxious, and I didn't want to go, but they assured us it would be helpful. We entered the Tavern, and immediately my heart rate elevated. We walked through the bar, the staff room, and the Dungeon, and whilst I was visibly shaken, and all those images of that night returned, we continued on. It was when we went to go into Pete's bar that I froze and succumbed to the fear.

The therapist said 'Kathy, why are you scared here? None of the robbery occurred here.'

I replied, 'But the stabbing did.'

All those visions of the blood-stained yellow shirt came flooding back. The therapist just had a look of shock and dismay, as no-one had made her aware of the stabbing one year earlier. We continued with group therapy for about six weeks, where we met other PTSD sufferers, and shared our stories. My husband also attended three days of therapy to help him better understand what I was going through, and what PTSD is. It really enabled him to learn how to assist me with my recovery, and it strengthened our relationship.

Living In Fear Of Enemies

I wrote the following four poems after the robbery.

To the Aussie Robber.

I know you're only a robber,
And that night you were full of beer.
I know you're out there somewhere,
And now I live in fear.

What made you do this to me?
I would really like to know.
Couldn't you hit the pub at night?
After you seen us go.

Did you really have to come in with guns,
And a balaclava on your head?
To scare the hell out of me,
And thought any second I was dead.

You're traumatized me to the max,
And one day you'll get your own.
You'll come a gutsa in the end,
And then you'll really groan.

Now I really hope you read this,
And hang it on your wall.
To remind you of what you've done,
Can't wait to see you fall.

From a Hurting Mind

The World In Which We Live

The world in which we live in,
Is not what it seems.
Just look at life as one more day,
For the next it could redeem.

I have three beautiful children,
But one has gone astray.
The drugs have taken over his life,
And taken him away.

I don't know what to do right now,
I feel I've had enough.
I do just have to realise,
That life is really tough.

My other two beautiful children,
Are seven and nearly five.
When they grow to teenagers,
I hope I'm not alive.

Myself, I've been in a robbery,
Not so very long ago.
Made me feel so close to death,
So close you wouldn't know.

I love my family very much,
But have to live in fear.
Of what could happen to all of them,
It makes me shed a tear.

This world in which we live in,
Is really getting bad.
Take it from me, one who knows,
Some days, you will be sad.

Kathleen Howie

The Lost World

I'm lost in this world
That I do not know.
Not a very nice world,
Which rocks too and fro.

It's a world of fear,
And it needs more attention.
It's a world of anger,
And this I must mention.

This world should be full of happiness,
Not sadness and heartbreaking.
And surely a lot of giving,
And not a lot of taking.

There is another world,
That is nicer and kind.
There is a way there,
That I have to find.

Kathleen Howie

Before It's Too Late

Again, I speak of robbery,
Thinking a bullet could've gone in my back.
Could've been dead so instantly,
Not even had time to pack.

I'd rather die of cancer,
At least I could've said goodbye.
One last kiss and cuddle,
And have a little cry.

I really would've hated it,
To have left my kin so quickly.
To think I could've gone in a second,
The thought is really sickly.

I wonder If I'd gone to hell,
Or up to the Pearly Gate.
I'm going to tell my kin every day,

I love them dearly,
Before it is too late.

Kathleen Howie

33. The Fall Out

After the robbery, I felt like my whole soul was ripped out of me. I no longer felt safe living in the city. These awful experiences just seem to be happening so many times, over and over, and over again. Like really, when is it going to stop.

Four months after the robbery, I had developed chronic PTSD, and I found it difficult to leave the house. I couldn't handle men staring at me for too long, as I either felt my make-up must be awful, or he is connected to the robbery somehow. Especially if he had blue eyes, and red eyebrows. Once, I heard a loud noise in the house and I froze. I screamed to my husband to check it out, and he discovered the golf clubs had fallen out of the cupboard in the room next to me. I felt like such an idiot. I was feeling really down about my life at that moment, as I wonder where it was going. I wanted to just up and leave this city. My husband had a wonderful job and had worked very hard to get to his position as a Manager. If we went back to Mackay, he would have to take a demotion, and reduced salary, and I wouldn't like to do that to him. I felt trapped.

Six months after the robbery, I felt like I had been chewed up and spat out. As staff, we had complained about several housekeeping issues, and safety concerns, however no-one had listened. I didn't even get a thank you for saving the poker machine money. This robbery has also unearthed bad memories of Sandra's stabbing eighteen months prior. I did not ask for this robbery to happen, and now I feel as if I am being punished. I lost my job. I couldn't work with money anymore. So much for me getting promoted to supervisor when my last child was off to school.

Whatever trust I had left in men had completely evaporated except for my rock, my husband. I was full of stress related dermatitis through my hair, and on my back. My seven year old son, Teale, had been experiencing horrific nightmares about us being robbed. He was terrified of going to sleep, in case these nightmares reappeared. If it didn't cease, I was going to seek some counselling for him.

Nine months after the robbery, and I was feeling like I shouldn't be there. At the robbery, I was running for my life so that I could live, and now I had lived through it, I wish I hadn't. A bit confusing to me. I went into survival mode to live, and now I wanted to die. My head was like a jumbled jigsaw puzzle that I couldn't put together.

I decided to do Folk Art classes at Spotlight, as a form of therapy. On one particular day, I went in to set up and put the kettle on. I then went to the toilet after washing my hands in the basin in the same room. I then went to open the door. Well, the door was locked. Panic set in, and what went through my mind was the terrifying feeling of everyone evacuating the building, because the kettle did not turn off by itself. My thoughts were of the fire alarm being set off, so I frantically bashed on the doors until someone came to rescue me. I was so scared, I couldn't breathe. I was looking for something to throw through the window. I even looked for cracks in the walls to get air. Finally, I was rescued by a passer-by. After I was out, I went straight outside to get some fresh air, and I sat down, and just sobbed uncontrollably. My husband had a conference at Couran Cove Resort, and we were all invited. Initially I said no, but soon realised I would be at home for three days by myself with the children. That was more terrifying than attending a conference. All I could imagine was a bunch of men in black pants and white shirts, which was what the robbers wore. I would be sitting there scanning the room for the robber's blue eyes and bushy red eyebrows, in a state of constant fear. I hid these thoughts from my husband, so he could enjoy his weekend.

Nightmares filled my slumber every night. One particular recurring nightmare was where all the staff were enclosed in room of glass, with a robber pointing a gun to our heads. In a room on the other side of the glass was the HR Manager, supervisors, and the police. The robber yelled hand over the money, or I will start shooting one at a time. They said they couldn't do anything about this, sorry, and turned their backs. I ran to the glass wall and banged furiously on the glass, begging them to give them the money. I was spread eagle on the glass wall, and as they walked off into the darkness, I slid down the glass wall sobbing. I awoke crying, which also woke my husband.

Kathy Howie

A Cry for Help.

The robbery has been a year gone by,
And I do keep wondering why.
I think of it all day long,
And always have a cry.

I wish I could have hypnosis,
To put it out of my mind,
Cause this is sending me crazy,
And a life I need to find.

I feel I'm trapped in a corner,
That is full of emotional fear.
Can't really talk about it,
No-one really wants to hear.

I try to keep this from my family,
And act so very brave.
But really deep down in my heart,
I want to hide inside a cave.

Kathleen Howie.

A Victim's Getaway

I'm a victim of a robbery,
And it's really hit me hard.
Now I am not working,
And sitting here like lard.

Cannot stop here anymore,
I'll have to get away.
Even if it's for a week,
I must just go in May.

I think I'll go up to Mackay,
A place where I was born.
A place to me that's really safe,
For here my mind is torn.

I'll go to see my friends,
And noises will not bug me.
I'll have a ball and just relax,
Up there no-one will shrug me.

I'm determined to get over this,
And know I surely could.
If I set off to Mackay,
It'll do me the world of good.

Kathleen Howie

34. Safe Town

I went back to Mackay by myself to get away from Brisbane, the robbery, and to assist with my recovery. I visited some of my favourite beaches, places, and friends, and I felt safe, and secure, and it was familiar. When I returned, I said to Rohan, I want to move back to Mackay. He had a wonderful job that he loved, and we had a beautiful home, but Mackay was where I felt safe. I was pretty selfish about the decision, but he knew it was the best thing for me, and he always said every time he went back to Mackay, it felt like home. The kids were at the right age as well, and it would not disrupt them too much. I did feel relief when I came back to my hometown of Mackay. I felt a lot safer, away from the big cities, and danger. For now!

We bought this house in Mackay, it wasn't the prettiest house, but it was secure. It had security screens on all the windows, and they were all lockable. It was a solid block home inside and out, so very strong, and possibly safe in cyclones.

Sixteen months since the robbery, and I was

back in Mackay feeling more at ease. I was off all my medication, however, I suffered withdrawal symptoms. The robber was still at large, and he was still a threat, as I could be a witness. I didn't have to constantly be on the lookout for the robber, as surely, he wouldn't follow me to Mackay. However, I was still fearful.

In my younger years, and prior to the robbery, I loved air travel, however, as a result of the PTSD, I was now so petrified of getting in a plane. I recall flying back to Mackay when we moved here with the kids, and I was so scared, and felt claustrophobic and confined. At forty-six years of age, I feel like I was a child again, and all those horrifying memories that I had tried to erase, had returned.

I had plenty of friends in Mackay, however, I had retreated into my shell, and didn't want to interact with anyone, as there would be questions. I was definitely not the person I used to be. I would keep curtains closed, and doors locked to protect me from the outside world. My fears started to affect my children's lives, as one afternoon my eight-year-old son, Teale, was sitting on the mailbox just watching the world go by, oblivious to any dangers. I had told him to come in, and we had an argument, and he lashed out, and said he hated me. I lashed back and told him he could be shot off the god damn thing, and that I had saved his life by getting him inside. I feel as though I was just being over-protective, but my children didn't see it that way.

June of that year, I had one of the most disturbing nightmares ever. In my slumber, my husband talked me into going back to work, and tried to be positive and said, "You are a strong person, and you can do it". While

I was working, these robbers came in like terrorists, and was holding us all hostage. One guy said to me he was going to rape my little girl, and I was going to watch. I went to my husband and told him I had to get the gun from him, and shoot my daughter, and then shoot myself so we didn't have to experience that terrible act. My husband was pissed, and didn't seem to care, so I took matters into my own hands to save my family. We ran downstairs, through laneways until we were all out. I got Teale and Madii on a motorbike and told them to ride as fast as they could. My husband and I were running after the children, and the next minute my children rode over this huge hill and into the sea. That's when I woke up balling my eyes out. It seemed that whatever I did to save them, it didn't work. I constantly had nightmares, and sometimes wished I could just cry alone.

Two years after the robbery, and I am feeling safer in Mackay, but only because I have protected myself from any danger. At times, it is difficult to control my actions, such as Bandana Day at the school to support cancer sufferers. All the kids had bandanas on their heads, and their faces. The kids wanted to wear them to school, but I flatly said no. The robber who chased me down the bar during the robbery had a bandana on. The kids didn't really understand. I went to pick the kids up, and all the other kids had bandanas. I turned to one child and yelled at him, "Just put a gun in your hand". I then raced home in anger and cut all my waist long hair off.

I still couldn't go to Bunnings, shopping centres or any other busy place. I didn't trust people I didn't know, and even people I did know, I was sick of the

Kathy Howie

comment, "Just get over it". My counsellor had told me to surround myself with positive people, not negative, or dumb people.

A nasty poem I wrote.

Dumb

Have you ever seen an ear bitten off,
And someone put it in your hand?
Blood bath all around you,
I guess you'll never understand.

Ever seen a friend get stabbed,
Five times in the guts?
Blood oozing from her shirt,
You probably cry at little cuts.

Ever been in a robbery,
And just waiting to be shot?
Looking at eyes through balaclavas,
No? I guess not.

I bet you walk down the street,
And do it without care,
Your mind is on all trivial shit,
As the wind blows through your hair.

I've had all this happen to me,
At the moment, I'm feeling numb.
I could explain all this in detail,
But thank god for you, you're dumb.

Kathleen Howie

Our house had low fences and gates across the front. The first thing I did was put six-foot high fences and lockable gates in. I just wanted to feel safe. Leave me alone people, don't come near me. We had to do the house up a bit, as it was just reasonable. It had pink carpet all the way through, brown linoleum floor in the kitchen, pink floral curtains. We painted the inside of the house white, put new white venetian blinds on the windows, with lovely calico drapes across the top and down the sides; nice brown carpet in the bedrooms; floating wooden floorboards throughout, except the kitchen, laundry, bathroom, and toilet, where we had white tiles. The kitchen had wooden lattice cupboards, and an orange bench top. Absolutely disgusting. Our backyard was full of gum trees, tea-trees, and fruit trees. We had become so accustomed to a pool in Brisbane, that we decided to cut down all the trees, and install a nine meter in-ground pool. The day after the trees were cut down, I was sitting on the back patio with a cup of tea, and thoughts started entering my mind. The cut off trees reflected my life as it was then.

Humans and Trees.

Humans are so vulnerable,
We're all so much like trees.
Standing, so proud of themselves,
Just swinging in the breeze.

It takes someone with a saw,
To take this all away.
Cut you down off your knees,
And on the ground you lay.

Cannot stand back on your feet,
Feeling hopeless and withdrawn.
Could have lived quite happily,
Not now my body is sawn.

Now I need to be replanted,
And hopefully grow again.
To make me big and strong one day,
And hope god can give me rain.

Kathleen Howie

35. Shock and Awe

We decided to get a new kitchen put in. We engaged the services of this cabinetmaker, who ripped out the whole kitchen, and put in lovely black marble laminated benchtops, with cream cupboards and drawers. We agreed on a stainless-steel splash-back, which went from one end of the kitchen to the other. It was very modern and stylish, at the time.

Two weeks after the kitchen was installed, we had a tiler commence laying tiles. The tiler had pulled out the dishwasher, and the fridge to lay tiles in those areas. We later found out there was an electrical cable that had been pierced by a screw and, also that the stainless-steel splash-back had not been earthed. When the tiler put the fridge and dishwasher back into their respective places, he unknowingly pushed the stainless steel onto the unearthed wire. When I came home from shopping with the kids, I found that the tiler had left an inch of dust all over the kitchen. It was everywhere. I picked up a wet rag from the sink and started wiping down the benches. I inadvertently touched the stainless steel with the wet rag, and it seemed to zap my fingers.

Feeling a bit weird, I threw the rag into the sink, and decided to have a cup of tea. Knowing that I shouldn't touch electricity with a wet hand, I reached over with my left hand, as the switch was in the corner of the kitchen. Instantly I am thrown back two metres. I was suddenly standing next to the fridge, with my heart in my throat, and wondering what had just happened. My kids were in the lounge watching TV, yelling out what happened to the TV? I went and turned the electricity back on, but I wasn't feeling well at all. I rang my husband, who was still at work, and he said to ring the electricity company, and that he was coming home right away. I then contacted Ergon, our electricity supplier. My daughter, meanwhile, was standing about one inch from the stainless steel. Ergon asked if there were any children in the house and I said yes. He said get them out straight away, so we dropped everything and rushed outside. I was sitting down in the carport looking at my children's faces, and they looked so scared. I was trying to act brave, because they were so scared. I had gone into shock and couldn't stop shaking. I was wobbling like a bowl of jelly. They were saying, "Mummy, you are so white". My heart was literally beating out of my chest and felt like it was in my throat.

Within minutes, the ambulance was there, then Ergon, then my husband. Then the tiler pulled up.

He said, 'What has happened?' He went on to say that he had received a shock in my kitchen earlier that day.

He had come back to warn me. Apparently, he had gone home, and when his dad came home, he told him about it, and his dad said we need to let them know, so they came back, but it was too late. I had already been electrocuted. Ergon checked the kitchen out, and they said the stainless steel was alive with 241 volts. I was placed in the ambulance, and taken to hospital, mainly for observation, to check that my heart rate, blood pressure and other vital signs were normal.

The next day I was released from hospital. I went home, and Ergon came around. I asked why would the splash-back be alive. We had just had a new kitchen installed. We later discovered that the cabinetmaker had decided to not engage an electrician to reinstate all the power points, and switches in order to save money. Ergon also said that if it was tiles instead of stainless steel, I would not have been electrocuted.

I was telling Ergon how I had turned the kettle on, leaning over with my left hand.

He looked at it and he said, 'When you turn that kettle on normally, do you hold onto the sink with your left hand?'

I said, 'Yes, normally, but my hand was wet.'

He said, 'If you had done that, you wouldn't be here today'.

The electricity would have gone from my left hand, to my right hand, straight across my heart. As it was, it went from my left middle finger to my right middle toe. I was so sick for days and weeks, as a result.

I found myself at the doctors every second day after the electrocution. I seemed to be alright laying down, with my head slightly tilted up. I was struggling to walk and maintain any sort of balance. Every time I went to the doctors, they were putting me on the heart machine, and blood pressure monitor.

I kept saying, 'It's not my heart, it's my head. I feel like I want to faint all the time.'

The Doctor kept saying, 'We have to keep checking your heart, because of an electrocution you can die up to two weeks later.'

After about three weeks, I was back at the doctors again!

I actually said, 'I was just dizzy'.

The doctor said that I had never once said that I was feeling dizzy. I had always said that I felt off, I feel sick, I feel faint. He was right; I had never said that I felt dizzy until now.

He said, 'I think I know what you have got.'

I started crying, thinking that at last, I was going to get better. He asked me to lay on the bed, he hung my head over the edge, turned my head to the left, then to the right, then straight ahead. He saw that my eyeballs were actually shaking. Oh, I was so sick after that. It is called the Hall Pike Manoeuvre. He diagnosed me with severe vertigo, and he sent me to see a Neurologist. He said my middle ear nerves had been singed from the electrocution, which can result in vertigo. Severe vertigo usually lasts up to ten months, but because of my situation it might be longer.

Living In Fear Of Enemies

Well, for three long years, on and off, I had severe vertigo, where I couldn't even walk to the toilet. One day I remember trying to crawl to the toilet, and I just ended up falling over, I couldn't even crawl. The longest I was bedridden was about two weeks at a time. During those times, I was thinking I was a wasted space. Rohan was there looking after me, again. I think the longest I could be up for was two days in a row, and then I would be back to bed again. I tried to be up out of bed as often as I could when the kids were home, so I could be there for them, however, I couldn't take them anywhere.

I never knew how long it would last, or when it would severely hit me again. I had to be on the bed with three pillows practically sitting up. I still suffer today from slight vertigo, but I don't get bedridden these days. There are different stages of vertigo. The doctor had said that once you get it, you will always suffer from it from time to time. You know I believe animals know when you are suffering from illness. We had a Burmese cat, Rani, who would always lay next to me on the bed, just within arms-reach, so I could pat her. Then when I could get up, and sit in the chair, she would lay on the arm of the chair. She was so comforting and kept me sane at times.

During my recovery from vertigo, and the electrocution, the police sergeant investigating the robbery contacted me, and advised me that they had captured the robber. I was so relieved. The ironic twist to this, was that the robber was an ex-police officer from Victoria. I kept paper clippings of these events that had traumatized my life. If he pleaded not guilty, then I was expected to testify in court, however, due to my vertigo I couldn't travel. They then said I could do a video link

Living In Fear Of Enemies

from Mackay, which terrified me, as I didn't want to look at him. It was all averted as he pleaded guilty and got eight years jail.

36. Unlucky Break

Everything was going fine.

A friend of mine was working as a Crossing Supervisor (Lolly Pop) lady for a school. She suggested that I try out to get a job there, as it was only for about one and a half hours in the morning and afternoon. Perfect I thought, but with my luck, I was worried I would be hit by a truck or a bus. I thought no, come on, and worked up the courage to apply, as I hadn't worked for many years. I was successful in getting the job, and I thoroughly enjoyed it, as I loved interacting with the little kids and getting them to cross the road safely.

Once again, I was contributing to society, but I was feeling very degraded, as the hospitality job I had had for twenty-seven years, and loved so much, was taken away because of the robbery. I did the job of a Lolly Pop lady for two years, until the school asked me if I wanted a cleaning job. I ended up a cleaner for eleven years. I loved the job but, at the same time, felt so degraded being a janitor. That's what life has dished me up.

In 2015 my daughter had her eighteenth birthday party. We decided to have it at home. We had a beautiful marquee out the back, disco lights, lots of food and games to play, and the pool was sparkling. Everything went fine. It was a fantastic night. We cut the cake, did the speeches, and settled into party mode.

Not long after that, I stood up and said, 'Come on, Maddi, let's dance.'

As I walked backward about four steps, I fell. I think the flashing disco lights had given me a bit of vertigo. It is the only reason I can think of that made me fall. On the way down to the ground, in my mind, it was like slow motion. Thinking to myself, I have to save my hips. I suffer with osteoporosis, and particularly in the hips. I threw my hands backwards behind me to save me. I hit the ground and the force snapped both my wrists in three places. Two bones in the right wrist, and one bone in the left wrist. My husband rushed over and helped me sit up and yelled out for someone to ring the ambulance and turn all the lights on. I sat there, with my hands all facing the wrong way. My husband tried to reassure me they weren't broken, but I think we both knew they were, just by their position. I looked up and my daughter, Maddi, started crying. The kids were saying, look at her hands. All the kids that had been under the marquee in the backyard, came running up to have a look at my hands. At least I was the center of attention for a change.

The Ambulance arrived, and Maddi was beside me crying and rubbing my back, and my husband on the other side holding my arms still. One of Maddi's friends wanted to be an ambulance driver. He was so good. He kept telling me to breathe. I think I turned him off being an ambulance driver. He actually changed his career direction after that night. Last time I saw him, he was working at a restaurant. They put me on the green whistle, which is a type of pain killer, secured both my wrists, and shuffled me into the ambulance. It totally killed the vibe of the party, and attendees either went home, or off to nightclubs.

My husband came with me to the hospital, and once I had been assessed, and booked in, and placed in a ward, he headed back home. I then had to have plates and screws put into both wrists. The party was on the Friday night, and I didn't get operated on until Sunday morning. The pain for the two days was shocking. I can't take morphine, as I am allergic to codeine. They put me on Endone. It was not enough to ease the pain. I was in hospital until the following Tuesday. Rohan had spent a lot of Saturday and Sunday with me, once he had packed everything up after the party and Teale, Maddi, and her friends all came in at various times to visit me, which was lovely.

On the Monday, Rohan said he would be back in the morning to see me and help feed me breakfast. Monday morning came around and they brought the breakfast around. I was starving by then. I had not eaten since Saturday lunch time, as they didn't know when they were going to operate on me. Rohan had to take everything back we had hired for the party, which took longer than he anticipated. Rohan naturally thought that the nurses would have fed me if he couldn't make it. So, there's this really nice-looking breakfast sitting in front of me, and I couldn't reach it, with both arms in splints. I couldn't pick up anything or squeeze anything. I couldn't even press the button to get the nurses attention. I started crying and thinking, where's Rohan. This lady in the next bed asked if I was okay.

I sobbed, 'No, I just want to eat something.'

She was so lovely. She dragged herself out of her sick bed and came and fed me.

I ended up asking this lovely lady next to me to press her buzzer whenever I needed anything. When I fell, I felt as though I might have injured my tailbone as well. It was so sore, but I did not want to tell anyone, because I didn't want plaster around my body as well. On one occasion I was trying to get off the hospital bed, but my tailbone was hurting so much, it was really hard and painful. I asked the nurse for help, and this rude nurse turned to me and said, "You do realise you are not the worst patient here you know". How rude; terrible nursing. I still didn't tell her about my tailbone. I was in so much pain with it.

I was released on Tuesday morning, and Rohan came to pick me up. Rohan had parked quite a distance away. The nurse had wheeled me down to the front of the hospital, while Rohan went to get the car. She sat me on the bench seat out the front, and just took off and left me there.

I was a bit scared because there was a car that pulled up in front of me, with this man in it. He was looking at me and smiling, and what was going through my head was, I can't fight anyone or push them away and he could just put me in his car and take off with me.

I was there for about five minutes before Rohan came back. I was so happy when I saw Rohan pull up.

Rohan looked irritated and said, 'I thought that the nurse was going to wait with you.'

I thought she would have done so as well.

So off I go home with both arms in splints, so you could imagine the conversation in the car between Rohan and myself. We were both thinking he was going to have to feed me, dress me, bathe me, take me to the toilet, everything we take for granted. My now eighteen-year-old daughter was absolutely brilliant looking after me. Rohan made the meals and cups of tea, dressed me, and operated the TV for me. Madii showered me for four weeks and helped me with the toilet for two weeks. So sad to think my eighteen-year-old daughter had to wipe my bum but did it without complaint. Teale couldn't bathe me or dress me, so he helped whenever he could with cups of tea and some meals and checking on my comfort levels. My eldest son so kindly offered to assist and come to Mackay, however, we felt I had enough people doting over me, and he had his family to look after.

I struggled a bit for the first two weeks, until I could at least feed myself and go to the toilet. After six weeks, I attended physiotherapy every two weeks, and it all came good except for sometimes the tendons would hook on the screws, and I would have to start wearing the braces again.

One day I was in the bank, and the teller had a

Kathy Howie

broken arm. She was commenting on my two broken arms, and I told her I had done it a year ago, but I had trouble with these tendons hooking on the screws. She said that she had the same thing happen to her. She went and had the plates and screws taken out. She said she felt a lot better, as now she can use her wrist and arm, even though her arm was still bandaged up from the second operation. She said her arm felt amazing. After that day, I decided to ring my doctor and get the plates and screws taken out. I did, two years after they had been put in. My arms felt so good. They are amazing now.

37. Living Life With a Few Bumps

The last three years had been pretty good. I had started travelling. I got the courage up to actually get on a plane. My second son, Teale, is an actor and had moved to Sydney, to establish himself, and build a career. In the same year, our daughter decided to move to Sydney and now attends UNSW (University of New South Wales). Our eldest son, Wayde, and his family, had lived in Brisbane for a long time now, and I visited them as well. My children living in major cities is daunting to me, however, it has given me the motivation to travel, and as long as I have Rohan by my side, I will always feel safe.

We decided to go and see one of Teale's shows at the Sydney Opera House. The show was amazing, and I was so proud to see him perform there. Our kids gave us a gift for Christmas, which was a trip on a Tall Ship sailing around Sydney Harbour. I am thinking no not doing it, but with Rohan, and the kid's encouragement, I got the courage up to go on that. Mind you, I had to have a fair few drinks beforehand to settle the nerves, prior to putting a foot on that boat, I have to admit. It ended up such a beautiful day, and a wonderful experience sailing around the harbour. You are in the middle of this huge city, and an extremely busy harbour, but the silence was incredible.

Experiences like that help erase all the bad images of my life and made me understand how lucky I was to have such a good life now, and a loving family. It seemed to calm me down before the next storm in my life hits. I know there is another storm coming somewhere, sometime, however I feel I am better prepared for it now.

My husband loves his sport and decided to get tickets for all of us to the NSW Open Tennis. I was so excited to go to the tennis at a big stadium on this trip and have a family day out. We got dressed in our best tennis attire, complete with large hats. We jumped on about three different trains to get there, so we could have a few drinks, and enjoy the day. We got off the train and immediately it started to lightly rain. We then had to get a courtesy bus to the actual stadium, which was nice, so we didn't have to walk in the rain. We arrived at the stadium, still filled with anticipation and excitement about the day, and the players we might see play. It was still raining so we found a nice little area to have a couple of drinks. The rain eased, so we went and sat in the stadium, and had something to eat just to embrace the atmosphere. The rain got heavier, and I am thinking, now what major stadium in Australia does not have a roof especially in a city like Sydney.

So, we then found and sat in this double decker bus that was made into a bar. We had an awesome day sitting there having a few drinks. We were about to leave when the rain finally stopped, and they got the court dry, so into the stadium we go and take our seats. The players came out warmed up, played two games and the rain came again. We hardly saw any tennis. It rained all day except for ten minutes. We decided that's it, we were going, as we had other things to do. Everyone was lined up at the ticket box to try and get their money back, but because they were going to play the tennis that night nobody could get a refund on their tickets. We just hopped back on the train and went home. At least we saw what the stadium looked like. The court was blue. Quite pretty.

The following year we went back to Sydney. I was so brave by now with flying, as I had got my courage back up. We stopped at the Bankstown Sporting Club. We stayed at the adjoining motel. It has an elevator as the motel is ten stories high. It was like a mini casino, with six themed restaurants. Absolutely gorgeous. We had a Christmas party there with friends of ours, who had come down from Brisbane. We were all staying in the same motel.

One day, I said to my friend, Debbie, that I had to go upstairs to put my phone on charge, and did she want to come up with me? She said, "No, I will wait here". I hopped in the lift by myself, which I don't usually like doing. I put my card on the panel and pressed the number eight, nothing happened. I did it again, and again, and again. I immediately started panicking. I rang Debbie and said the doors won't open. I am locked in this elevator. Half of the elevator is glass. Debbie was there looking at me through the glass trying to calm me down. She was yelling at security to help. She did say that this is the wrong person that this can happen to.

Kathy Howie

I could hear the security at the door trying to open it. I heard one guy say to another guy, we haven't got the key to this elevator, and the company was in Melbourne. By then, I was feeling like I had run out of air, and I couldn't breathe.

I just slowly sat down on my bum, with my phone beside me, trying to calm myself down by saying, it's alright, Kathy. There was a pond around the lift with koi fish in it. Debbie was trying to take my mind off the situation by telling me to look at the fish. I was at my wits end by then. I just stood up, and I grabbed the doors, and with all my strength, I opened them about two inches, and I could see three sets of hands the other side helping me get out. I squeezed out. I wasn't crying before, as I think I was in shock, but once I was out of that door I just cried and cried. Debbie was holding me. I will never ever get in an elevator again. Deb and I went to the bar, and then Rohan and Debbie's husband turned up, (they had been taking one of the hire cars back to the airport, and Debbie had phoned Rohan and told him what was happening), and I got absolutely blind drunk. I reckon I drank a carton of beer that night. Everyone said it could only happen to you.

The next year, we went down to Sydney again. We stayed at this lovely little motel with no lifts. Rohan made sure when he booked it, that there were no lifts. It was really close to the airport, and the train station. We thought we would not hire a car this time, make a real holiday out of it. No fighting the hustle and bustle of the traffic, and just use public transport. One day we went into the city, did a tour around the harbour on the ferries, went to the Opera Bar, just did the tourist thing.

We were coming back to the motel by train. A little bit of a hill that we had to walk up. Next minute this guy is running past us. He said I wouldn't go up there if I were you, there was a madman running around with a knife! He was saying his girlfriend was screaming, that was my girlfriend. We could hear screams coming from the other side of the train line. We heard someone again say that there was someone running around with a knife.

We slowly kept walking up the hill. The road was blocked off with police tape. We saw two police vehicles, a big forensic van, and the police were not letting anyone through. We could see our motel on the other side of the taped off area.

I said, 'We are just staying there at that motel.'

It was then that I looked on the road, and there was a white sheet over a body. I said to Rohan, there was someone there, they are dead. I went into panic mode again. I immediately said to Rohan that we had to get out of there, so we went back down the hill, and hopped on the train, and went and got off at one station down the track which meant a longer walk back to our motel, but safer.

This station just happened to be the station that our son and daughter used, as it was close to their apartment. They were both at work, so we decided to go to a pub close to the station and have a drink and wait for the kids to turn up.

Once again, I got stuck into the beers, and ended

up a bit merry. I don't often drink beer, but I must think beer is a good solution for anxiety, as lately that is what I have done every time there is a traumatic event in my life. It's a wonder I am not an alcoholic.

I said to Rohan, 'I am not going back to the motel just yet, that madman with the knife might be trapped in there.'

This is what was going through my head. Madii turned up from work, and she said it was all over the news about this stabbing in Arncliffe.

On the news, it said that this guy had stolen a Woolworths van, rammed into two cop cars, plus other cars. This happened about five suburbs away. There was a big cop chase through the streets, until two suburbs away, he got out and stole a red taxi. He dragged the taxi driver out of his car and stabbed him and stole the taxi. The chase was still on, until he got to Arncliffe, until he got right out the front of our motel. There he was cornered near the motel. The police cars came in from either end of the street. This drug fuelled idiot decided to jump out of the taxi and he committed suicide. I naturally thought thank goodness for that, he didn't hurt anyone else. The taxi driver survived and was released from hospital.

Now, how big is Sydney, is this a big city or what? In all of Sydney, he has to murder himself out the front of my motel. Life just likes to give me a little reminder of its fragility, and to keep me on my toes. Life can't go that smooth for me, can it? The crime scene was blocked off all night. By seven pm, Rohan rang the motel, and they said we couldn't get in the main entrance, but they have opened the fire escape doors for access, which was just around the corner, out of sight of the crime scene, and there were not any police tapes there. We had dinner at the restaurant on the balcony looking over the crime scene, police lights flashing. We retired to our room, and went to bed, the police lights were flickering through our curtains all night, as they had a police car parked right outside our window.

You would think that I would never go back to Sydney again. My husband is my rock, and continues to encourage me to embrace life, and new experiences. The following year we went back to Sydney, and saw some live shows, like Billy Elliot and Kinky Boots. We did a couple of other big trips. We travelled a lot that year. We went to Melbourne; in the middle of winter I might add. Saw a game of AFL at the MCG, went to the Vic Arts Centre, to see the Terracotta warriors, and visited friends and family.

We then travelled to Perth and Bunbury, for a mate's fiftieth. We saw Quokkas on Rottnest Island, and dolphins in the Swan River. We travelled to Brisbane a couple of times to visit our oldest son and his family and took the grand kids to Sea World. We also went on a three-day comedy cruise with friends, just to test it out, as it was our first cruise. I didn't use the lifts, so had to walk up and down numerous flights of stairs, but we had plenty of time. Believe it or not, nothing bad happened on any of those trips, and I had the most amazing times, and have wonderful memories. Maybe, just maybe, maybe, maybe, my life might run a little bit smoother, and I can continue to enjoy some of life's great experiences. Who knows, maybe an overseas trip one-day?

Epilogue

I retired on the February 14, 2020, and I am now enjoying spending my time with my rock, my wonderful, patient and understanding husband. Travelling to new places and enjoying visits with my beautiful children and grandchildren.

I am now sixty-three years of age, at the time of writing, and have survived into my twilight years. Never thought I would make it past twenty-seven. Life is still throwing a few curve balls, but life is good. It is the year of the COVID-19 Virus (2020), which has impacted all our lives, however, it has not affected me too much, but has touched the world with devastating effect.

My proudest, and biggest achievements of my life have been raising my three beautiful children; Wayde, Teale and Maddison.

Since I met my husband, every incident that had happened to me, he would say, "You should write a book". So, after about twenty requests and suggestions, I have finally written my story. I was always nervous to tell my story, as I was terrified of reliving those awful memories. It has taken five years, but I have made it. My past is now a closed book, and hopefully never to be relived again.

This is why I have had time to reflect on my life, and decided to finally tell my story

This is my story, a story of a child who was abandoned, sexually abused and unwanted. At times I felt as though there was no escape, and that this would be my life forever. I was then accepted by a foster mother, who taught me to be a lady, and a father who did a wonderful job to raise me, eventually. It is a story of a young woman who fell in love, but it was never reciprocated, and ended in abuse, and once again abandonment. Resulting in drug abuse and suicidal thoughts.

The joy of being a mother, and then marrying a wonderful husband, who loved and protected me. Then stabbings, robberies, electrocutions, and vertigo causing, further damage to my already bruised mind.

This is my story, and I hope by me writing about my experiences, it will inspire others to tell their story. People who have been in similar circumstances, or people dealing with mental health issues from horrific childhood scars of the past. There is a light at the end of the tunnel, and there can be happiness in your life.

Let me complete my life to date by saying that my story started as;

L.I.F.E.

"Living In Fear of Enemies".

I now understand it is,

"Love In Family is Everything".

ABOUT THE AUTHOR

A Journey of heartbreak, violence and survival.

This is a story of a young child that was tossed from pillar to post. Chuck and shut.

No real home to survive a world of dangerous crossroads.

A Survivor of child abuse, abandonment, entrapment, victim of a robbery, a witness to horrific violence.

She felt powerless, worthless and useless to anyone who crossed her path.